A Practical
Guide for
Starting an
Adult
Faith
Formation
Program

D0109386

Resource Publications, Inc.
San Jose, California

Reprint Department
Resource Publications, Inc.
160 E. Virginia St. #290
San Jose, California 95112-5876
(408) 286-8505
(408) 287-8748 fax

Library of Congress Cataloging-in-Publication Data

Brown, Richard C., 1935-
    A practical guide for starting an adult faith formation program / Richard C. Brown.
    p. cm.
    Includes bibliographical references.
    ISBN 0-89390-572-0
    1. Catholic Church—Adult education. 2. Catechetics—Catholic Church.
    3. Christian education of adults. I. Title

BX921.B76 2003
268'.434—dc21

                                       2002037138

Printed in the United States of America
03 04 05 06 07 | 5 4 3 2 1

Production staff: Nelson Estarija, Romina Saha, Elizabeth Gebelein, Susan Carter

For Theresa and Bruce, Ken and Susan,
Tony and the Beasleys, and especially Paulette,
for their support and wisdom over the years.

Contents

Foreword

I recently attended the planning session for a Diocesan Priests Convocation. We were asked to share issues and topics about which we felt passionate. I have to say that two items at the top of my list would have to be (1) the parish and (2) adult faith formation. For the vast majority of Catholics, their experience of church, for good or ill, is practically co-terminus with their experience of parish. Congressman Tip O'Neill liked to say that all politics are local; our spirituality and religion are local as well. The experience, vigor, and vitality of church depend largely upon the experience, vigor, and vitality of the local parish community. Chancery office, diocesan departments, bishops, and even the Vatican may well be in the average Catholic's vocabulary, but the experience of church is almost entirely the experience of parish.

Past generations of Catholics may have grown up in a community and culture that sufficiently conveyed all they needed to receive about being Catholic. Family, relatives, neighbors, parish life with novenas, devotions, sodalities and societies, the strong impact of parochial schools, and even an anti-Catholic culture, all converged to arm earlier generations of Catholics with considerable information, education, and formation. In that bygone era, new questions did not continually assault the believing Catholic from both beyond and within the church as they do today.

We live in a society where almost everything is questioned. Why should we be surprised if this also applies to the topic of religion and to issues of faith? More and more we are questioned and challenged to justify and articulate our religious beliefs. And we must do so for ourselves. Many would describe this not as secular attack or unbelieving critique but as a basic element of healthy adult faith development. At infant baptisms, I often remark that every child has the right to be baptized and raised in a faith "which they will probably reject as teenagers and hopefully come home to as adults." Because the world is a context to our faith and we, as human beings, are its subject, the homecoming is a lifelong process.

In my own parish experience, we have featured adult education evenings with speakers and discussion. Topics have included Bible study, religion and science, internal church issues, and best-selling books. We have developed a support system and resource material for large numbers of small church communities. We make available on tape and on-line all adult education sessions as well as each weekend's homilies. We have recently added Bishop Ken Untener's suggestion of a four-minute post-communion teaching at Sunday Masses. Our catechumenate community is effective with both candidates and sponsors. With all that, my assessment is that we do not go deep enough, reach out enough, or include enough issues of parishioners. And many parish communities offer considerably less.

Another judgment from my pastoral experience is that academic study, advanced learning, and professional scholarship, crucial and important as they may be, are not our goal nor are they sufficient. Adult faith development means personal reflection in community and repossession of the truths we cherish in the ever shifting context of our lives, our society, and our world. Education must lead to formation, formation to ministry and ministry to mission; and then we will not only grow as adults but as disciples rooted in Jesus, living in the church and world of the twenty-first century.

There is no "one size fits all" answer to the challenge of adult faith formation. And there is no community that "has it all together." With this book, Dr. Brown offers a vision and strategies to link parish life and adult formation from which we can all profit.

Brian T. Joyce
Pastor, Christ the King Parish
Pleasant Hill, Calif.
Former Diocesan Director
of Adult Education for the Diocese of Oakland, Calif.

Acknowledgments

Reprinted from *Our Hearts Were Burning Within Us* © 1999 United States Catholic Conference, Inc. Washington, D.C. Used with permission. All rights reserved. No part of this document may be reproduced in any way without permission in writing from the copyright holder.

The Holy Bible: New Revised Standard Version, © 1989, Division of Christian Education of the National Council of the Churches of Christ in the United States of America. Nashville, Tenn.: Thomas Nelson, Inc. Used by permission. All rights reserved.

Excerpts from *The Collected Works of St. John of the Cross.* Translated by Kieran Kavanaugh, OCD, and Otilio Rodriguez, OCD © 1991 by the Washington Province of Discalced Carmelite Friars; and from *The Collected Works of St. Teresa of Avila, Volume Two.* Translated by Otilio Rodriguez, OCD, and Kieran Kavanaugh, OCD © 1980 by the Washington Province of Discalced Carmelite Friars. www.icspublications.org.

Excerpts from *Excellent Catholic Parishes: The Guide to Best Places and Practices* by Paul Wilkes © 2001. Used with permission of Paulist Press. www.paulistpress.com.

How Do You Make the U.S. Bishops' Vision Happen?

When a pastor asked me a few years ago to start an adult faith formation program from scratch, I recognized a man of vision. Here stood someone who understood the need and right for all adults to grow in their personal relationship with God. Sunday Mass, though of prime importance, was not enough.

Within a year, we had 1,500 adult parishioners attending a variety of three-session adult faith formation seminars (mostly at $15 per person—a figure arrived at by the parishioners themselves to help fund the new program). Some seminars drew two hundred people, but most were in the range of thirty-five to seventy. Through the U.S. census, we also found 2,500 Hispanics within our parish boundaries, but only fifty attended Sunday Masses. I gave a seminar on "Hispanics in the U.S. Church," based on the U.S. bishops' pastoral letter of 1983, *The Hispanic Presence: Challenge and Commitment.* All twenty-two participants in that seminar joined as leaders in a new Hispanic ministry. They soon turned out five hundred Hispanics for the parish's first Spanish Mass.

The moral of this story is that every parish is hungry for so much more for adults. We must do for adults what we are doing for children and teens. The time for adults has come.

The U.S. bishops are responding to this need. Their vision produced a dramatic call for adult faith formation in their November 1999 document *Our Hearts Were Burning Within Us.* They deeply desire all adults to experience a personal relationship with God that develops throughout their lifetime.

What possible forms can this adult faith formation program take? Lifetime adult catechesis might include:

- the study of Scripture to learn more about God and how to respond to the word.

- the study of the social teachings of the church and how to build a just society in which all God's children can thrive.

- preparation for church liturgy and sacraments to better experience the growing fullness of a personal and community relationship with God.

- opportunities to relate faith to the personal, family, church, or social situations of one's current life.

- spiritual formation experiences, such as new forms of talking with God, discerning God's movement in one's life, and following Christ's example.

- systematic theological instruction to better understand one's faith and to develop the skills to share it.

All of these opportunities enable adults to fulfill Christ's summary of what their human lives are all about: "You shall love the Lord your God with all your heart, and with all your soul, and with all your mind. This is the greatest and first commandment. And a second is like it: "You shall love your neighbor as yourself" (Mt 22:37).

Numbers Do Count!

Another moral of the above story, and a conviction of my own, is that numbers do count. I firmly believe that God expects us to be concerned about numbers. A current cultural belief in our U.S. church ministries is: "You do the best you can in church ministry but don't worry about how many people turn out." Rather, I think God is concerned about all his children, about each and every one of us. Why would God hope that only a few people attend an adult faith formation seminar? At the heart of your ministries should be the conviction that you can and must reach all your people. This requires your programs to be excellent and your marketing to be the latest in what works to attract people. Numbers, for the sake of all God's adults, do matter!

What Do the Bishops Say?

Throughout the first three parts of *Our Hearts Were Burning Within Us*, the bishops discuss adult catechesis, which promotes a lifelong growth in an adult's personal relationship with God. The topic pops up again and again as they compel us to see adult faith formation as the new priority for all parishes. They describe the mature Christian adult. They describe content and delivery approaches. But their most striking focus is adult catechesis—what actually works in bringing us to truly know, love, and serve God. Part IV describes the organizational structure that every parish and diocese needs for effective adult catechesis.

As you explore how to start your parish program, refer to Parts I–III. In the introduction, "A Renewed Commitment to Adult Faith Formation," the most helpful sections include a description of how Jesus catechized adults at Emmaus (7–15). The list of referred documents, which includes the *General Directory for Catechesis*, offers a wealth of concrete suggestions for your program. There is also a list of challenges and concerns facing the church (32–37), including problems such as human dignity, family stress, the limited faith experiences of many Catholics, people leaving the church, and some catechetical efforts falling short.

In Part II, "Qualities of Mature Adult Faith and Discipleship," a bulleted list instructs how to maintain a life of union with Jesus (51). Characteristics of mature faith are described (52–63), including recognizing that "however great or modest our competence or accomplishments, God's favor is always a gift and a grace" (63).

Part III, "A Plan for Ministry: The Goals, Principles, Content, and Approaches for Adult Faith Formation," contains lists that are concrete and helpful. One of the three "principles" (75–87) for conducting adult faith formation is to "use the catechumenate [*Rite of Christian Initiation of Adults*] as an inspiring model for all catechesis (Cf. GDC, nos. 59, 68, 88–91)" (81). When the bishops explain the six "dimensions " of Christian life (88–96), they write that one aspect of a dimension is learning how to "live a lifestyle reflecting scriptural values of holiness, simplicity, and compassion" (93). The bishops also explore five "concrete approaches" (97–112) for achieving adult faith formation. In a description of one of the approaches, "Family- or Home-Centered Activities," the bishops assert that "catechetical opportunities situated in family settings foster both adult and family faith growth, while also addressing one of the major reasons adults give for not participating in adult education: time away from their families" (103).

How Is Adult Catechesis the Key to Adult Faith Formation?

Adult catechesis is the most important skill described by the bishops in their document; it is what they flesh out in Parts I–III. Adult catechesis is also the primary skill needed by the adult faith formation leader, the adult faith formation team, the catechists of adults team, and their counterparts at the diocesan level.

At the center of adult catechesis is the development of a personal relationship with God as expressed in service. But for all adults, how practical is the goal of developing this personal relationship with God? In real life, every adult experiences a need to be happy and to cope with life. Some find both in TV, sex, power, wealth, travel, and good food, and that is as far as they get. Others go further and find happiness and purpose primarily in love relationships. But every adult, given the opportunity, can also experience a more deep-seated curiosity and hunger for an ongoing and growing personal relationship with God. Given the opportunity, adults marvel at God's loving and intelligent presence in every created thing around us. Given the opportunity, they marvel at how God personally loves and powerfully acts in their lives day after day. Opportunities for reflecting on and responding in love to God's presence and wisdom in their daily lives are what we, as church, must provide.

Considering adult catechesis as a skill, one of the most typical ways to achieve this lifelong conversion to God is by connecting Scripture to adults' personal daily lives. You can walk into a Mass and hear a sermon that makes a personal connection between the day's Scripture and your daily life. On the other hand, if the sermon is merely a theological tract, it is not likely to achieve its primary catechetical function. One of the bishops' more powerful statements on adult catechesis is that we need to lead adults to a "deeper appropriation of the Gospel and its power to guide, transform, and fulfill our lives" (52).

An Example of Connecting Real Life to Scripture

Recently, in a parish seminar called "The Parents of Jesus," we read the story of Mary and Joseph losing the teenage Jesus in Jerusalem I asked the mothers of children in the catechetical classes what experience they personally had of momentarily losing a child. Silence. Then a hand tentatively rose, and a mother spoke.

"I dropped my eleven-year-old daughter off at a friend's birthday party at an amusement park. I said I would pick her up at 5:00 P.M. When I returned at 5:00 P.M., she wasn't with her friends. I was very worried. I prayed. It took me half an hour to find my daughter in another part of the large park with one of her friends."

I asked the mother, "What did you first say to her?"

"I said, 'How could you do this to me? I've been worried sick as to what might have happened to you!'"

"And did you get an answer?" I asked.

"My daughter said something about how she and her friend just got carried away, having such a good time together. I figured it was something I would have to think about."

I asked, "Do you realize how similar your reaction was to how Mary reacted? You were very worried. You asked her for an explanation. You told her how worried you were. You decided you needed to ponder her explanation. Every element was exactly how Mary dealt with her teenager in the temple. See how well God knows and sympathizes with our real problems, such as our teens experiencing their own uniqueness and needing their peer relationships."

"I know," the mother said. "I could feel the connections happening as I told you my story!"

There are so many opportunities to connect adults to God's presence in their lives through the use of Scripture.

How Did Jesus Catechize?

Jesus, God incarnate, catechized adults with impressive skill. For example, Jesus was the model catechist with the two disciples at Emmaus. Like Jesus, you must join people in their daily concerns, ask questions, and listen attentively to their joys, hopes, grief, and anxieties. Then share the word of God and unfold the meaning of their experiences in light of Scripture, God's messages to us about existence. Trust the capacity of prayer and sacrament to open adults' eyes to the presence and love of Christ. Then invite them to live and share this good news.

Earlier in Jesus' ministry is another example of his method of adult catechesis. Jesus connected with the Samaritan woman at Jacob's well through her physical thirst and her divorces. He dealt with her in a warm, friendly manner. He let her experience God's non-condemning, personal concern for her. He drew her up from daily life to what is really important—the kingdom of God among us—through her experience of thirst and need for water. Later, she went off to serve others by telling them this central message of life, that here is the savior that God promised us, who is the loving God in the flesh.

The bishops in their document reflect that "in Jesus the disciples caught a glimpse into the heart of God," as did the Samaritan woman (11). Though the bishops do not include in their document the behavior of Jesus with the Samaritan woman, the story is strikingly similar to Jesus' steps in catechizing the disciples at Emmaus. Among the steps, the use of bread at Emmaus and water at the well reminds us how much God uses physical things as a medium for grace. The sacraments prove God's love of this medium.

An illustration of this occurred for me when a seventeen-year-old boy on confirmation retreat told me how he had written out his problems on a sheet of paper, which he tossed into the fireplace. As he watched the paper burn, he was overcome with the awareness that, in the years ahead, only his relationship with God would be of importance and all else in life would be as ash.

Bishops' Call for Adult Catechesis That Touches Real Life

The bishops offer specific suggestions for adult catechesis in their document. "Start by listening to adults and let the stories of their lives and the hungers of their hearts inspire pastoral care and inform catechetical programming ... (Cf. GDC, nos. 189–190)" (80).

The call for the parish adult needs assessment at the heart of adult faith formation. The bishops are specific: "*Respect the different learning styles and needs of participants, treating adults like adults, respecting their experience, and actively involving them in the learning process*" (82).

I recently sat in on the opening of a parish adult seminar on baptism. First, the priest asked the participants what they had personally experienced regarding baptism and what they felt about those experiences. Only then did he go on to his theological and scriptural description of baptism, all the while staying open to the participants' questions and reactions. He had them start the evening by forming a circle of chairs, facilitating their sharing and sense of community, of family. Adult catechesis actively connects with adults' lives.

What remains most striking in the document descriptions regarding adult catechesis is that service to others makes catechesis happen! The bishops call for us to engage adults in the life and ministry of the community. "'Adults do not grow in faith primarily by learning concepts, but by sharing the life of the Christian community' (ACCC, no. 28). Not that concepts are irrelevant; they are foundational. But for most people the truths of faith really come alive and bear fruit when tested and put into practice—in soup kitchens, neighborhoods, small groups, workplaces, community organizations, and family homes" (83).

That certainly puts theology classes into perspective in adult catechesis. Teaching theology without connecting to the lives of the participants is just not the way Jesus catechized adults.

Applications to Other Parish Ministries

Like adult faith formation, all parish ministries dealing with adults can respond with enthusiasm to the U.S. bishops' document *Our Hearts Were Burning Within Us*. Which aspects of the document in particular are relevant to other ministries?

Adult catechesis skills are of primary value. These skills include personalizing adults' relationship with God, connecting their lives to Scripture, working toward personal transformation in their attitudes and behavior, and other elements reflecting the model of Jesus' way of catechizing. Also of importance is understanding and using adult psychology, which provides insight into how adults learn and skill in identifying individual talents and sources of motivation. Other aspects of the document relevant to all ministries include adult spirituality, service, and community building.

Another issue for other parish ministries dealing with adults is the U.S. bishops' desire that the entire parish work toward developing an adult faith formation paradigm. For example, how can the parish prepare elementary-age children and teens for lifelong adult faith formation? One answer lies in connecting their real-life issues with Scripture through dialogue, as you do with adults. This will effect a personal transformation in young people's loving relationship with God.

Now Trust Your Vision

What remains the most important issue as you start an adult faith formation program in your parish? You must trust your vision. Keep asking yourself and like-spirited souls, "What will work in this new ministry of ours?" Continually look for and experiment with answers to this question. Trust your judgment and that of the Holy Spirit who wants to guide you in the most important task of today's church. Persistently ask for God's strength and light to guide you in your work. Speak up and share your vision. You can quickly enflame the whole parish with your passion. In the words of Paul Wilkes in *Excellent Catholic Parishes,* "What the vast majority of Catholic parishes lack is not priests or resources, but vision, energy and hope."

Choosing and Training Leaders

No task surfaces as more important than choosing and training the adult faith formation director, the governing team, and the catechists of adults team. Both pastors and the diocese are responsible for choosing and training adult faith formation directors who have the necessary skills to train their teams in turn.

The Pastor Chooses the Adult Faith Formation Director

What skills and qualities does a pastor look for as he searches for an adult faith formation director? This person, who will be responsible for the entire program for adults, should have many skills and qualities. For example, a candidate with a gregarious, sociable personality gives the pastor reassurance that the many new relationships needed for this program will happen. The adult faith formation director also needs to be intelligent, articulate, organized, and creative. Of additional importance is a director's ability to perceive the pastor's feelings and the ability to accurately respond to them. The ability of the director to discern how people are feeling is the skill of counseling—a major key to the success of the program.

The most important learned skill the director needs is a growing knowledge of how to do adult catechesis. This represents the primary concern and contribution of the whole adult faith formation program. The background to support this adult catechesis skill would ideally be a master's degree in theology or pastoral theology. Also desirable would be training in one or more of the following areas that support adult catechesis: adult education, counseling, and spiritual direction.

The adult faith formation director must be a dynamic leader and must possess speaking skills to present the program to the parish and volunteers. While the promotional skills can come from parish volunteers, skill in volunteer development must come from a director.

In hiring a director, the pastor should feel that this prospective director is well-organized, flexible as opposed to rigid, and most especially, emotionally healthy. A reasonable final consideration is whether or not this person has a prayer life. The Holy Spirit needs someone open to the input of grace, whether that input comes through his or her own wisdom, through the pastor, or other members of the Body.

Where Does the New Director Start?

How does a new adult faith formation director start from scratch? First, you must recognize which parish ministries are most effective. Meeting with the directors or coordinators individually—over lunch or breakfast—within the first two weeks will accomplish the following important goals:

- They will know you care about their great wisdom and vision concerning the needs of the adult parishioners.

- They will come to know you as a person they can work with in the future, as you begin to bond.

- They will know you trust their judgment because you asked for it, and they will begin trusting your judgment.

Because you praise the helpful information, insights, and vision they provide, they will be prepared to support and praise your vision for this new adult faith formation program.

On the other hand, you will now see the limitations and potential problems that need to be dealt with in the future. You have also begun relationships for your own emotional support in the stressful but exciting days ahead.

In the parish where I started an adult faith formation program from scratch, those first weeks of interviewing current staff members, besides producing all the above results, also gave us nine speakers for the adult catechesis program. My question to the staff was "What theology, Scripture, or other topic would you most like to teach if you had the chance and if you thought there was a need?" Out of their choices, there was an excellent match with the major topics later chosen by the parishioners.

The Director and Pastor Relationship

The next important job for the director, besides the selection of team members, is to establish an ongoing relationship with the pastor. Some examples of this include discussing visions for this program, asking the pastor to share his vision with the parish, and gaining his support for the program's various initiatives. On the director's part, a quarterly report to the pastor with a list of what the director and teams have accomplished provides objective proof that the pastor's investment is paying off. Also of benefit is the pastor's support of the director's appearance before the congregation, often during the first months of this new parish ministry. This can be done before or after Mass or as a lead-in to the Sunday announcements. Many pastors already provide this kind of opportunity to the director of youth ministry at the Mass for teenagers.

Chapter 2

What Are the Tasks of the Director?

Hiring an adult faith formation director requires justification for this full-time position. What will the director do to justify being hired? Adult catechesis is the primary responsibility and contribution. The director accomplishes this through the ongoing development and use of the adult faith formation governing team and the catechists of adults team.

Secondly, the director, through his or her teams and his or her own activity, provides a parish program of seminars, small faith-building groups, classes for parents of children in catechesis, and other adult catechesis opportunities. Examples of small faith-building groups could include Bible study, small faith groups, and group spiritual direction. The director and his or her teams must assess the needs of the parish and surrounding community, develop programs that respond to those needs, and then find multiple ongoing ways of marketing the program's vision and all its activities.

Besides these direct adult faith formation program activities, a third major area of the director's responsibility is seen in contributions to the other adult ministries of the parish. Examples include helping in the training of volunteer teachers of children's catechesis, catechumenate adult volunteer groups, catechists of the parents of infant baptism classes, catechists of teen confirmation classes and retreats, and the pastoral care ministry volunteer team. This latter area of assistance could include other groups of volunteer adults that help out in other ministries. The focus would be to catechize these adults who, in turn, will catechize, or bring into a closer relationship with God, the children, teens, or adults that are the subjects of these other ministries.

A fourth area of the director's work includes volunteer development. The director's skill, shared with staff and volunteers alike, reflects concern for identifying, attracting, correctly placing, and maintaining adult volunteers. This concern relates to the theological principle that baptism calls every Catholic to a service somewhere, including within the church itself. Also, with the background in adult catechesis, psychology, and education, the director of adult faith formation has a role as trainer in catechizing prospective and current volunteer adults in the call to serve God.

However, every ministry in the parish needs to develop and maintain its own group of volunteers. The director of adult faith formation cannot be a director of volunteers for the whole parish. Not only is there not enough time for that but also the director of each ministry is responsible for developing and maintaining ties with his or her own volunteers.

The director has the above tasks, namely, to develop the two teams of adult faith formation and the programs for which they are responsible. He or she must also extend the skill of adult catechesis and volunteer development to all parish ministries involved with adults.

The director's fifth task is to constantly assume responsibility for assisting the pastor in the overall spiritual development of all parishioners. Whatever contributes to the deepening of the parishioners' personal relationship with God and its expression through service to one another and in the wider community remains a constant question and life concern for the director of adult faith formation. All parishioners, including children and teens, must be a focus of the program because the adults provide the atmosphere and modeling for their children's religious growth.

The director also has a sixth task or responsibility—attending parish staff meetings. These meetings provide the director with regular opportunities for giving input about the progress of the adult faith formation program. In addition, opportunities for applying adult catechesis, marketing, and volunteer development to other ministries will present themselves. Also possible are spontaneous reactions from the director relating to a vision of adult needs and rational, common sense dealings with parish situations.

Selecting the Teams

The major responsibility of the adult faith formation director, besides having ongoing discussions with the pastor and staff, is to select members of the adult faith formation team and the catechists of adults team. The first team represents an advisory, decision-making, and governing board for the entire program.

The first set of skills and qualities required of members represents what every member of both teams needs: a decision maker. Besides decision making, necessary skills and qualities include sociability, organization, responsibility, logical intelligence, intuitive intelligence, artistic intelligence, counseling, nurturance, flexibility, tolerance, and emotional health.

A helpful first step for choosing parishioners with these desired abilities is to give the following descriptions to the pastor and staff at a meeting. Afterward, ask them to suggest names of people to contact as potential team members.

The twelve skills you are looking for in the members of your adult faith formation team and the catechists of the adults team are:

1. **Decision making:** This represents the most obvious, the most easily discerned skill of the natural leader. You see this person, male or female, as a take-charge person. They enjoy being leaders, whether they are making decisions, initiating conversation, or directing an entire group.

2. **Sociability:** A person with this quality is outgoing and gregarious, whether in one-on-one encounters or in a large group.

3. **Organization:** Orderliness reflects the behavior of one who is organized. He or she likes to follow a schedule and prefers to keep each possession in its own rightful place.

4. **Responsibility:** Highly disciplined, the responsible person completes each task efficiently, yet thoroughly.

5. **Logic intelligence:** Step-by-step processing reflects a logical person's intellectual approach to problem solving.

6. **Intuitive intelligence:** This problem-solving approach reflects a quick, intuitive, independent rush to a solution.

7. **Artistic intelligence:** Intellect as applied to creating beauty reflects this quality, whether in music, art, design, dance, or strong appreciation of physical beauty.

8. **Counseling:** You may repress your anger but a person with this skill perceives how you truly feel.

9. **Nurturance:** A nurturing person knows how to respond to the emotional and physical needs of others. He or she delights in helping other people.

10. **Flexibility:** Rather than being attached to a few set principles of life as touchstones for all decisions, a flexible person enjoys judging each situation on its own unique merits.

11. **Tolerance:** Others may shun people who are different but the tolerant person enjoys reaching out with friendliness to those who are different.

12. **Emotional health:** Someone who is emotionally healthy remains peaceful as opposed to anxious.

This set of skills and qualities required of every team member creates both a positive challenge and some difficulties. The positive challenge, of course, resides in finding a full team of people with all these talents. But you need all of these skills and qualities in your group. The most critical need is that every single team member should strike you as emotionally healthy. That will provide for the greatest productivity and the least difficulty in the team's work.

The most typical difficulty arising from these skills comes from having more than one decision maker. Each decision maker enjoys having things work out based on his or her judgment, resulting in possible clashes with other decision makers in the group. However, with all the work there is to do, you need as many decision makers as possible.

The selection of team members must include people of different ages, races, economics and other descriptors of adult parishioners. In their document, the bishops insist on this demographic mix.

Second Set of Skills for the Adult Faith Formation Team

This second set of skills relates only to the first team, the adult faith formation governing team. Perhaps each member possesses only one talent but the team as a whole must have a wide variety of special talents. Additional skills needed by the adult faith formation program team are in marketing, volunteer development, theological training, public speaking, finance, social service, adult and family counseling, and legislative expertise for outreach ministry. The more of these skills each team member brings to the table, the better.

Adult catechesis is a skill that primarily resides in the director, who in turn is responsible for training all members of both teams. It is always helpful to have on the adult faith formation team additional members who are experts in this capacity. You will need team members who possess skills and experience in the following six areas:

1. **Marketing:** Marketing and advertising skills account for the numbers of adults God expects you to reach. All God's adults are important. Proper marketing brings in many more than otherwise would respond. "Grace builds on nature," as St. Thomas Aquinas wisely stated.

2. **Volunteer development:** A comprehensive adult faith formation program, with its different ministries, requires many skilled volunteers. The program is responsible for training or assisting other parish ministries in their own volunteer programs.

3. **Theology, liturgy, and spirituality (including spiritual direction):** Adult catechesis requires all the theological, liturgical, and spiritual information and skills at its disposal. Someone with a master's degree in theology can provide this continual input.

4. **Adult and family counseling:** A volunteer with a master's degree in counseling would enjoy giving general input on adult psychology as well as marketing to adult needs. This person can also assist in forming a volunteer group of certified counselors for the parish's adult and family needs.

5. **Legislative and legal expertise (for outreach):** Every parish should include in its adult service a legislative team to help deal with the social issues in the city, county, and state. An attorney familiar with legislative activity could create and manage such a team for the parish.

6. **Social services (for outreach):** Someone with a master's degree in social work would have the background and wisdom to help develop the many outreach services to meet the needs of both the adult parishioners and the broader community.

Second Set of Skills for the Catechists of Adults Team

The catechists of adults team provides the program with its many seminars, workshops, retreats, and other adult catechesis opportunities. These opportunities involve skills in teaching, discussion, questioning, group process, theological reflection, discernment, and so forth, but most especially the overall skill of adult catechesis. However, each member should come to the team with at least a degree in theology and experience in adult education or public speaking.

Issues and Projects for Team Training

Having brought the two teams together, the director must next deal with the goals of developing a vision and resolving conflicts. Without an overall vision of which adult faith formation needs should be addressed the most in the parish and wider community, a tremendous waste of time easily occurs in the months and years ahead. Some questions that can help the team develop a parish vision are:

- Why are we here?

- What is this ministry all about?

- What is church all about?

- What is God's kingdom all about?

- What adult faith formation needs do we see in this parish?

Besides developing a vision, resolving conflict remains of great importance in developing an effective team. The primary source of conflict exists in the natural differences between the positive God-given talents of the members of the team.

The following are additional training issues and projects for the director to deal with in team meetings:

- Have the pastor describe his vision for the adult faith formation program. Discuss how the U.S. bishops' *Our Hearts Were Burning Within Us* applies to your own parish.

- Present and discuss adult catechesis. Discuss the need for general seminars, small group offerings, service opportunities, liturgy, and other forms of adult catechesis.

- Develop a needs assessment plan, including a written survey, small-group discussion, and individual interviewing possibilities. Present feedback you received in interviewing all the parish ministry directors regarding the adult needs they see.

- Discuss marketing and advertising principles and applications.

- Discuss how to invite, place, and maintain volunteers; consider program needs and which parishioners might be invited to join the teams.

- Discuss the action of the Holy Spirit in the team meetings. Encourage all to speak up when they feel impelled to, when the material is relevant and the time appropriate, and explain how members need to listen to what all other team members have to say.

- Develop plans for a hospitable experience—that includes refreshments—at all program events.

At the Diocesan Level

The recommended skills of both the director and the adult faith formation teams also apply at the diocesan level. Whether or not the diocese creates the catechists of adults team, individual parishes should form these teams with the degreed and talented parishioners already present among them. Some dioceses across the United States have already developed catechists of adults teams in order to provide either diocesan-wide, regional, or individual parish seminars for adults.

Another option for dioceses would be to have their own team of experts in adult catechesis that could train catechists of adults teams in each parish, rather than have the parish adult faith formation director be solely responsible for that training.

Applications to Other Parish Ministries

If your parish does not have an adult faith formation director, here are some suggestions for getting started. Someone on the parish staff may need to assume the responsibility of initially calling for volunteers for at least the adult faith formation team. Training can begin with the "Issues and Projects for Team Training" of this chapter, then volunteers can proceed to Chapters 3–10. For example, following a pace of two- to three-hour modules for each chapter, at one module per week, you can complete the training in two months. During training, the members can develop actual plans for the parish program over the coming months.

The skills listed in "Selecting the Teams" apply to any ministry group's volunteers. Many of the points discussed in "Issues and Projects for Team Training" have applications in developing volunteer groups for the various ministries.

The very concept of teamwork merits emphasis. Do volunteers in any ministry feel isolated in performing their assignment, or do they experience themselves as part of a team? They may need to re-vision their ministry together and experience family. Also, within the team, separate areas of responsibility help alleviate natural issues of control created by drawing together so many natural leaders.

Because the team provides a ready-made Christian community, your volunteers in every ministry will experience the reality of being the family of God.

Chapter 3

What Is Adult Catechesis?

One day I had a chance conversation with a bright eighty-year-old lady from Prescott, Arizona, as we waited for our cars to be repaired. After listening for a while to her current woes, I decided to meet my writer's need of the moment. I asked, "What most helped you develop your personal relationship with God over the years?"

She quickly responded, "The hardships of my life. The Lord helped me. I couldn't have survived without his support. Otherwise, it would be a hollow life."

"Anything else?" I asked.

"Yes, I always talk with him as though he is sitting across the kitchen table from me, but I have never seen any shining light come down! I thank my parents who got me [to go] to church, [where I learned] there is a God to pray to."

This pioneer woman became, for me, additional proof of how God is looking in every adult for the opportunity to catechize, to establish, or to deepen a personal relationship.

How Jesus Catechized at Emmaus and the Well

Jesus himself worked at building this relationship with God at Emmaus after the Resurrection (Lk 24:13–35) and with the Samaritan woman at Jacob's well (Jn 4:5–42). That is, Christ shows us how to conduct adult catechesis. The comparison between Jesus' behavior at Emmaus and his manner of dealing with the Samaritan woman at Jacob's well reveals seven steps for catechizing adults.

First, there is an especially important step in starting the adult catechesis process. In order to help people develop their personal relationship with God, begin by letting them talk about the current situations in their lives. Does this happen in the normal theological seminar in the parish? Much observation would suggest it does not happen very often. Jesus demonstrated exactly how to connect with adults' current life situations.

On the way to Emmaus, Jesus' first question to the disciples is: "What are you discussing with each other while you walk along?" (Lk 24:17). He directly engages them at that moment when the disciples are "discussing" (Lk 24:15) what had happened during the past three days. When they question his awareness of the "things that have taken place" (Lk 24:18) with Jesus of Nazareth, he prompts them again to share their experiences and feelings by asking, "What things?" (Lk 24:19). Twice he asks the two disciples to share what they had experienced regarding the recent death and resurrection of the Jesus they had known.

Jesus does the same with the Samaritan woman. He directly engages her, saying as she comes to the well to draw water, "Give me a drink" (Jn 4:7). When she questions how he can share a drink with a Samaritan—an unacceptable behavior for a Jew—he draws her into the reality of her relationship with God. He shows how God is present in her life by telling her he knows about her string of husbands and current lover. He encourages her to pursue a more intimate relationship with God: "Worship the Father in spirit and truth, for the Father seeks such as these to worship him" (Jn 4: 23). Throughout their discussion, he connects the truths of God's personal relationship with her to the current facts of her life, using both the water she had come to draw and her male-female relationships.

Both at Emmaus and at Jacob's well, Jesus shared Scripture, God's words, God's relationship with us. At Emmaus, he went through Scripture to show how all they had experienced was what God had promised in the Old Testament. To the Samaritan woman, he reflected on the living water symbolism found in the Old Testament.

Besides connecting with adults through Scripture and relating life to Scripture, there are two additional aspects of adult catechesis that bring us into a deeper relationship with God: sacrament and service. Sacrament is God's way of connecting with us in physical ways, dealing

with our five senses as mediums for his grace or love. Whether it is
baptism with its water, oil and flame, or communion with bread and
wine, God connects with us through physical signs of his presence.
At Emmaus, Jesus ends by breaking bread with the disciples, blessing
them with an awareness of his presence. Only then did they recognize
who he was and said, "Were not our hearts burning within us while he
was talking to us on the road, while he was opening the scriptures to
us?" (Lk 24:32). And with the Samaritan woman, Jesus uses his drink
of water to symbolize her relationship with God. He tells her, "The
water that I will give will become in them a spring of water gushing
up to eternal life" (Jn 4:14).

Besides sacrament, service is also a major part of adult catechesis.
Mary, the mother of Jesus, once rushed to provide service to her
cousin, Elizabeth, who was in her sixth month of pregnancy. This
was after Mary encountered God's messenger and the Holy Spirit at
Nazareth (Lk 1:26–45). At Emmaus, the two disciples got up on their
own and immediately went to Jerusalem. There, they told what had
happened and how they experienced Christ, in the breaking of the
bread. Their service to the apostles and the other disciples was in
sharing their encounter with God. How similar was the reaction of the
Samaritan woman in her encounter with Christ. She also hurriedly left,
leaving behind her water jar. She went to her city in response to God's
love and gave herself in service by telling them of her encounter with
the Messiah. This extraordinary woman may have been the first of
Jesus' most effective missionaries.

There is a sixth step in Jesus' method of adult catechesis. Building
community or hospitality through the breaking of bread at Emmaus
and the sharing of drink at Jacob's well are not by chance. Relationships
are built around food and drink, whether at a family gathering at
Easter—a highlight of the year for many—or a cup of coffee on a first
date. Refreshments should never be forgotten at an adult catechesis
event.

Another observation about building community or hospitality is that
the two disciples at Emmaus no doubt provided the bread, as they
invited Jesus to stay with them. And the Samaritan woman provided
the drink, saying, "Sir, you have no bucket" (Jn 4:11). Adults also need

to bring the refreshments as their contribution to building their relationship with God and one another in catechesis. In your relationship with him, God needs your contribution of what you can do, what you can provide.

It is fascinating that Jesus covered so much, but the only mention of prayer is in his blessing of the bread at Emmaus, which could well have been "give us this day our daily bread" (Mt 6:11). And with the Samaritan woman, he did speak of worshiping the Father. Yet at Emmaus and at Jacob's well, the disciples and the Samaritan woman were involved in the best of prayer. They were in a constant personal dialogue with Jesus, their God.

How to Apply the Seven Steps of Jesus' Catechesis

Jesus' catechizing at Emmaus and at Jacob's well apply to seven principles of adult catechesis that you can use in your work. Begin by following these steps:

1. **Start with adults' current life situations.** Always establish a connection between yourself and their present circumstances—in what they are doing and feeling right now—throughout the catechetical process.

2. **Use Scripture.** Consider God's personal conversation with us as a mandatory medium to include in catechetical situations. Use Scripture from the liturgical cycle of the week or day at every catechetical event.

3. **Connect Scripture to adults' current life situations.** Always connect Scripture and theology (the study of God and our relationship with God) with their current life experiences and feelings.

4. **Connect with sacrament.** Use physical symbols of God's truth and love as often as possible. Continually connect adults with the sacraments and other liturgy.

5. **Connect with service to others.** Adults need some form of service or outreach as an expression of their personal love relationship with God. Community building and hospitality are major expressions of this service.

6. **Share food or drink.** Building hospitality and community happen around food and drink. By bringing the refreshments, adults make their contribution to the catechesis event.

7. **Include personal prayer.** Personally talking with Jesus best reflects what happened at Emmaus and Jacob's well. Whether in silence or in sharing, this and other forms of prayer with Jesus (or the Father or the Holy Spirit or Mary or the saints or the angels) need to happen in every adult catechesis event.

The Theology of Adult Catechesis

What is adult catechesis? First of all, adult catechesis enables adults to grow in their personal relationship with God. Such a purpose finds its roots in the primary purpose of adult life: to know, love, and serve God and your neighbors as yourself.

God created for you everlasting love relationships with the three persons of the Trinity and with one another. You have this time on earth to either exercise your freedom and contribute as a human being or to do nothing. If you make a free contribution of your loving gifts to God, others, and yourself, you have personally achieved honor and value for which you can feel satisfied for the rest of your eternal existence. You have freely made this contribution in response to God's love.

Now, what does this mean in relation to adult catechesis? Adult catechesis is the process of enabling people to enter into and to develop their own love relationship with God. This relationship is lived out in service to others and yourself.

Does Jesus at Emmaus and Jacob's well achieve this definition of adult catechesis? Does Jesus enable the disciples and the Samaritan woman to enter into and form their own love relationship with God? Jesus powerfully brought the Samaritan woman into what life is all about, a personal relationship with the Father whom we must worship in spirit and truth. She also brought this reality to her fellow citizens who overwhelmingly responded to Jesus.

At Emmaus, Jesus was working with the disciples who knew the God-man personally. Jesus brings together all of their experiences with him and their familiarity with God with his valid claim, "Oh, how foolish you are, and how slow of heart to believe all that the prophets have declared!" (Lk 24:25). In other words, see how God loves you! Here I am! Or as he concluded, in talking about God as spirit to the Samaritan woman, "I am he, the one who is speaking to you" (Jn 4:26).

This should remind us that Jesus is our best medium for bringing adults into a personal relationship with God. The concrete connection between their personal existence as humans and the person of God in Jesus remains the best way—the sacramental, physical way to catechize. The miracles that occurred through Mary and the saints throughout church history are additional signs of God's appreciation of our need for a sacramental means of connecting with him.

Simple Method of Relating to God through Scripture

To bring adults into a growing relationship with God, offer a simple way to enter into prayer or dialogue with God through Scripture. An adaptation of a method developed by Father Steve Tutas, the former international Superior General of the Society of Mary (Marianists), includes the following steps:

1. Select a Gospel passage of interest that relates to something you are dealing with or are concerned about in your life. For example, if you experience difficulty with a co-worker over a difference of judgment about how to handle a work situation, you might use the following passage between Jesus and Mary at the Cana wedding: "When the wine gave out, the mother of Jesus said to him, 'They have no wine.' And Jesus said to her, 'Woman, what concern is that to you and to me? My hour has not yet come.' His mother said to the servants, 'Do whatever he tells you.' Now standing there were six stone water jars for the Jewish rites of purification, each holding twenty or thirty gallons. Jesus said to them, 'Fill the jars with water.' [After the steward had tasted some, he said,] 'But you have kept the good wine until now'" (Jn 2:3–10).

2. Having selected the passage, read through it slowly, circling or underlining the words, phrases or sentences that strike you or convey God's message most powerfully. God communicates with you as you read the Gospel.

3. Answer the following three questions in your response to God:

   • What is God saying to me personally in this Gospel?

   • What will I do in response to what God is saying to me?

   • How do I convert "what I will do" into a prayer of petition to God?

This simple exercise can be used daily as the primary method of maintaining a personal dialogue with God. It is an example of what an adult faith formation director can introduce to adults in many different catechesis situations, such as adult faith formation seminars.

A Sample Seminar:
Applying the Steps of Jesus' Catechesis

The following seminar, "Parents of Jesus: The Best of Child and Teen Parenting," was an experiment in adult catechesis that I presented as a six-week series. Refer to this seminar when practicing adult catechesis. You can also use the seminar as an adult catechesis model for creating your own adult faith formation seminars on many other topics.

The Parents of Jesus: The Best of Child and Teen Parenting

Step One: "Start with parents' current life situations." Provide the participants with a three-by-five-inch file card and pencil to respond to the question: "What currently concerns you most regarding your child(ren)?" And then ask them to get together in pairs or small groups to share any concerns they choose.

Step Two: "Use Scripture." Refer to Scripture passages of Mary and Joseph dealing with Jesus, their son.

Step Three: "Connect Scripture with current life situations." Apply the Scripture to the participants' parenting situations. Present each of the following passages as an exercise.

> 1. Luke 1:26–55: Mary accepts and rejoices in having a child. She shares her joy with her cousin Elizabeth. *Application:* How do we, as parents, accept and love our children? How do we nurture relationships within our family?

2. Matthew 1:18–25 and 2:13–23: After learning that Mary is with child, Joseph fears that he and Mary will be condemned by the public if they marry. An angel warns Joseph that Herod plans to find and kill the Christ child. Joseph, Mary, and Jesus flee to Egypt. *Application:* How do we handle fear in ourselves and in our children?

3. Luke 2:21–39: Mary and Joseph bring the baby Jesus to the temple. Simeon and Anna greet the baby Jesus and foretell the greatness of his ministry. *Application:* How do we handle religious experiences for our children? How do we respond to input from others about our children?

4. Luke 2:41–51: Mary and Joseph lose the twelve-year-old Jesus in Jerusalem. Three days later, they find him in the temple, conversing with the teachers. Mary and Joseph express their concern for his well-being. *Application:* How do we deal with our teens who want to find their own unique identity and be socially accepted by peers, which are their two primary developmental tasks?

5. John 2:2–11: Mary and Jesus disagree at the wedding of Cana. Mary urges Jesus to reveal his glory by performing a miracle with wine, but he hesitates. Later, he performs the miracle and gains the trust of his disciples. *Application:* How do we handle trusting our own judgment and teach our children to trust theirs?

6. John 19:25–27: Mary supports Jesus throughout his ministry and until his death on the cross. *Application:* How should we maintain our relationship with our grown children?

Step Four: "Connect with sacrament." This requires a great deal of creativity. Look for sacramentals—physical things that stimulate any of the five senses—to become signs and conveyors of God's graces, presence, or activity. Some examples throughout the seminar include:

paper and pencil through which the Holy Spirit inspires people to write new ideas, questions, or insights; the participants' own copies of the Bible, through which God speaks to them; their words to each other as they share, respond, or listen to how God is active in their lives.

Sacramentals could also include: 1) pictures of relatives; 2) plane ticket stubs or other souvenirs of a family move; 3) their children's baptismal or first communion certificates, or a birthday card with a message from a relative; 4) career test results from a teen or the personality inventory results from observations of their children; 5) water and wine; or 6) souvenirs such as company logo tee shirts, from their grown child's career.

Step Five: "Connect with service to others." This can include community building by mingling with them as they arrive. Afterward, you can encourage them to stay for further conversation to get to know one another and see where they might help each another.

Step Six: "Share food or drink." Have participants volunteer to bring refreshments to each seminar session, providing healthy alternatives. Hold a final evening's potluck meal at one of their homes.

Step Seven: "Include personal prayer." Open and close each session with a prayer circle that includes spontaneous prayer and encouragement for individual petitions and thanksgiving. Soft worship music from a recorder before and after the session allows group conversation but provides another very important element of prayer experience.

What Adult Catechesis Is Not

There are three different historical definitions of adult catechesis. First, catechesis is defined as instruction through which adults receive the knowledge and skills necessary for being an active member. Second, adult catechesis is described as formation, the process by which an adult is brought into the community by sharing its stories, rituals, and way of life. True adult catechesis occurs when adults examine their beliefs on the religious topics at hand to see why they hold those beliefs. It happens when they form a connection between what they are taught and their growing lives as Christians. This best occurs when adults share their experiences and insights in open discussion with one another, personally reflecting on the topic's application to their lives.

The catechist is only one source of the Holy Spirit working through everyone. Adult catechesis is a time of personal theological reflection that brings about living the kingdom of God as true evangelizers.

Applications to Other Parish Ministries

Most parish ministries are involved with adults they can catechize, whether they be the volunteers themselves or the clients of their service. For example, children's catechesis programs often have their directors and adult volunteer catechists work with parents. Liturgy, catechumenate, St. Vincent de Paul, small faith communities, teen programs, pastoral care, parish social events and Bible-sharing—the list of ministries having the mission and opportunity to catechize adult parishioners goes on and on.

Do the ways in which you deal with adults catechize them as the U.S. bishops call you to do? Whether they are parents, volunteers, or the clients of your ministry, do they grow in their personal relationship with God? This is the purpose of catechesis. Adults should enjoy opportunities to relate with one another, to experience life in God's loving family. As instruments of God's love, they profit from opportunities to serve others, including their own families. They experience God's love in many ways through others but do you take advantage of the seven ways Jesus used to catechize, bringing them into a growing personal relationship with God? Like Jesus, you must get to know your adults in their real lives, connect them with God's response in Scripture through dialogue, and enjoy with them the working of God's grace as they experience change in their attitude, behavior, and service.

Chapter 4

Match Talents to Program Needs

In all my years of identifying ministry talents in people, the two leaders who most reflected the skills needed for ministry were Marilyn and Edward. Marilyn led more than one thousand Hispanic leaders. Her skills created a magnificent level of energy and enthusiasm among all her leaders. Edward led a brand new Hispanic ministry of twenty-two leaders. He possessed great skill in understanding and drawing out all the skills of his team.

In Marilyn's case, the entire diocese benefited from her ministry. In Edward's case, as his team discovered they could create a Hispanic ministry, its dynamism became a sign of hope for Hispanics in other parishes. Both Marilyn and Edward symbolized for me what power there is in matching natural God-given skills with the needs God has for ministry.

How Did Jesus View Talents and Ministry?

Jesus summarized his overall message from the Father, the truths of the kingdom, in the parable of the talents. The master gave his slaves "talents," "each according to his ability," before he left them. Most of the slaves went out and shared their talents with others. Afterward, the master returned and demanded an account of their success. He praised those who had invested, thereby multiplying, their talents. But he cast out the unproductive slave who had buried his talent (Mt 25:14–30).

God, our master, wants us to serve one another by sharing the talents he has given us. But how do we multiply them? As an example, if God gave me the gift of counseling and you received the gift of strong leadership, we will benefit from one another's gifts by sharing those talents in service to one another. We multiply the talents we possess by sharing one another's.

The history of the ancient Hohokam Indians of Phoenix, Ariz., revealed to me a powerful example of how the multiplying of gifts is an expression of fulfilling God's will for us. I was writing this book at a picnic table in South Mountain Park, Phoenix, the largest mountain city park anywhere in the United States. Suddenly, I noticed rock art on the cliffs and boulders all around me: a huge lizard on the face of one cliff, a lone deer on a boulder, a small lizard dancing with a human stick figure on a second boulder. Another mass of petroglyphs, which helped the Indians calculate God's solstice and equinox, appeared on a group of boulders. All, I learned, were part of a major religious center for up to as many as fifty thousand Hohokams living there from 40 A.D. to the 1400s.

Did the Hohokam spirituality include sharing their talents with each other in service? Indeed, they built the largest canal system in the world, one that still delivers water to provide food through fields of agriculture in the Valley of the Sun today. They traded their craft and artistic talents across the Southwest, in Mexico and California. They traded religious frog figures that they uniquely etched from California seashells, using rosin and acid. Their religious rock art also reflects a culture rooted in spirituality, a deep reliance on and appreciation of God's power in nature. Today, we continue this instinctive sharing of talents in service to others out of love for God.

Someone might question my using the word "talents" in the parable to mean personality or psychological skills. However, there seems no other logical explanation for the talents to which Jesus refers. For twenty-five years, I have examined psychological systems that attempt to describe the human personality. All of the systems use skills or talents to define specific personality types.

"To one he gave five talents, to another two, to another one, to each according to his ability"(Mt 25:15). The different number of talents that Jesus refers to is a way of saying that each one of us receives a unique set of talents. In the makeup of each human person whom God created, there is only one set of characteristics that a) one has from the master, b) that can be shared with others, or c) that one will be held accountable for when the Lord and master returns.

Talents Also Tell Us God's Will for Our Lives

An additional bonus about this question of God-given talents is the reality that God makes it simple for us to know his will for our lives. If we identify and use our unique set of talents, we live according to God's will. We do not have to ask God constantly, "What do you want me to do with my life?" Nor do we have to hang around waiting for answers.

Enjoyment Tells Us What Our Talents Are

If our talents reveal to us what God wants us to do with our lives, how do we know what talents God gave us? And how do we match our God-given talents with our adult faith formation ministry?

God gives us the ability to identify our talents. God created us in such a way that our talents automatically produce enjoyment when we use them. Our psychological experiences of what we enjoy and what we do not enjoy tell us what our talents are. The enjoyment, in turn, provides the motivation to use that talent again and again until our lives are over and we have fulfilled God's unique purpose for us. Enjoyment gets the job done. For example, the team member with a talent for teaching adults derives enjoyment from teaching, motivating him or her to continue to grow in ministry. This service helps others and helps the teacher to enjoy his or her existence—both of which God intended.

Let it be noted, however, that to enjoy a talent does not refer to the enjoyment that can come from sitting back and doing nothing. We are talking of enjoyment that happens during or as a direct consequence of using your talents. However, as most work may involve the exertion of effort or even suffering from boredom, using our talents may not always be pure enjoyment. It may be enjoyment mixed with the cross.

Talents in Ministry Are Important

All of the reflections about the parable of the talents underscore the importance of talents in ministry. Utilizing the talents of your ministry team does not happen haphazardly. You do not assume a leadership role unless you have the natural talent for it. Nor do you dump any live body into a volunteer slot. Identifying talents or skills rests on solid theology. We want adult faith formation leaders to fill the slots God made them for, so that they will be totally motivated and full of joy.

The list of skills, as applied to leadership in adult faith formation ministry, includes at least the following twelve: decision making, sociability, organization, responsibility, logical intelligence, intuitive intelligence, artistic intelligence, counseling, nurturance, flexibility, tolerance, and emotional health. I developed this list and the questionnaire that follows from more than twenty-five years of analysis and research on the talents of leadership, but their roots lie in Edwin Megargee's research and testing as found in his *California Psychological Inventory Handbook*.

A Self-Evaluation of Your Talents

On a three-by-five-inch file card, write either the numbers one through twelve, or write out the names of each of the following twelve talents or skills. For each skill, rate your level of proficiency and enjoyment, marking as follows:

S: for **Strongly,** if the overall description of the skill describes what you strongly or usually enjoy doing and/or strongly or usually do well;

O: for **Occasionally,** if the overall description describes what you occasionally or sometimes enjoy and/or sometimes do well;

R: for **Rarely,** if the overall description describes what you rarely or never enjoy and/or rarely or never do well.

Special Note: Please give yourself the S, O, or R rating that fits the majority of descriptions for that skill. Now, rate yourself on these twelve skills or talents:

1. **Decision making:** I have the skill to take the initiative and lead others. I easily make decisions. I talk more than I listen. I influence others. I trust my own judgment. I am a take-charge person. I enjoy people who accept my decisions, judgments, and opinions. I carry through on what needs to be done. I will speak up and tell others what I think.

2. **Sociability:** I feel poised and self-assured in dealing with others. I handle group situations in a relaxed and confident manner. I do not have irrational feelings of rejection being with a group of people. I enjoy social interactions. Light conversation is easy for me. I am outgoing and gregarious.

3. **Organization:** I am organized. I prepare in detail for my work. I love to keep everything in its proper place. I tend to listen to others' needs to the detriment of my own needs. I restrain myself from irrational behavior in general. I rely on thought and reason to solve problems. I shun impulsive or anti-social behavior.

4. **Responsibility:** I accept responsibility for a task and carry it out to its conclusion. I am conscientious, dependable, and govern my life by reason. I believe in attention to duty and in disciplining myself. I am consistent and orderly in my behavior. I do not have any addictions.

5. **Logical intelligence:** I enjoy thinking in a step-by-step, logical fashion. I am organized in my thinking, speaking, writing, and problem-solving. I enjoyed schoolwork, particularly algebra. I am a diligent worker who plans ahead. I accept rules and regulations. I do not enjoy people who are confused or superstitious. I prefer logic to solve problems as opposed to quick answers.

6. **Intuitive intelligence:** I excel in situations that require independent thought and creativity. I reject simple authoritarian attitudes, such as "There is only one right answer to any question." I think for myself. I am an original thinker who can come up with new solutions, new ideas, and new directions.

7. **Artistic intelligence:** I enjoy watching, listening to, or participating in one or more of the following: music, drama, or dance. I enjoy forms of intelligence applied to the creation of something beautiful. I enjoy the beauty of God's outdoors. I enjoy poetry. I do not like to abide by strict rules and regulations.

8. **Counseling:** I enjoy perceiving other people's feelings, needs, and concerns. I discern other people's feelings, even when they have not expressed how they feel. I am observant and perceptive. I have a natural ability to counsel others; people come to me with their problems. I like to be with people who discern my feelings.

9. **Nurturance:** I am responsive to the needs of others, especially regarding their physical and emotional needs. I like to share feelings and to be physically affectionate. I enjoy fixing meals for others. I am hospitable and warm towards others. I prefer to give rather than to receive.

10. **Flexibility:** I see each new situation or person I encounter as unique. I believe there can be more than one right answer to a question. I do not enjoy arguments over matters of principle. I am flexible rather than rigid or dogmatic. I am excitable. I do not enjoy being with people who follow only a few set principles in life, rather than judging each situation on its own merit.

11. **Tolerance:** I am open to personalities different from my own. I am forgiving, benevolent, considerate, charitable, non-sexist, and non-racist. I am accepting and non-judgmental of others regarding their beliefs and attitudes. I do not hold resentment or hostility toward others. I am trustful and confident rather than cynical and suspicious. I am comfortable with people different than myself.

12. **Emotional health:** I feel peaceful rather than anxious. I enjoy keeping a rational and positive outlook on life. I feel comfortable with who I am. I enjoy each day, doing the things that I like to do and do well. I do not suffer from back pain or constant headaches that may be psychosomatic. I am able to concentrate on the tasks at hand. I expect to succeed in the things I do. I care what happens to me.

Following your assessment, those skills marked with an "S" rating are your strong points. You can depend on those skills to represent God's will for you and to fulfill your use in ministry. The more your ministry requires those skills, the more you will enjoy it and be motivated to work hard. Skills rated with an "O" will also be helpful to your work. The "R" ratings are work skills you may want to avoid and that you can delegate to others.

Talents Match Program Needs

The next task is to compare each of the above leadership talents or skills with the needs of the adult faith formation program. From this list of talents and the matching needs of the program, it would seem that everyone needs all the following skills to the greatest extent possible. This includes the director, the adult faith formation team in their teamwork, each individual member of the team in their own areas of responsibility, and each catechist of adults.

1. **Decision making:** All leaders need to make decisions for the adult faith formation program to progress.

2. **Sociability:** Successful team meetings and all group situations, including seminars, liturgy, social outreach projects or other events require leaders who have mastered this skill. Hospitality and community building are a major part of this ministry.

3. **Organization:** All the leaders must organize people, events, or ideas. In doing so, they need to draw on the resources of other people's ideas, needs, and strengths.

4. **Responsibility:** Very little will happen in this ministry if the leaders do not carry out their tasks to the end. Procrastination stifles the productivity of the program.

5. **Logical intelligence:** Ministry vision, planning, marketing, problem-solving, production, and evaluation require a constant logical review of facts bound together with rational conclusions and action.

6. **Intuitive intelligence:** When leaders act on creative intuition, the program will flourish. Leaders should also seek creative solutions to difficult ministry problems, such as finding new ways to market or to resolve a leadership conflict.

7. **Artistic intelligence:** This skill is most needed in liturgy. But there are many other applications, such as any event involving music, dance or drama, or a community-building potluck that needs decorations.

8. **Counseling:** In adult faith formation you deal with the needs of adults. This intuitive skill proves valuable, whether in catechizing them, providing group spiritual direction, marketing to their needs, or more clearly understanding them in any situation.

9. **Nurturance:** A leader must respond in outreach to the physical and emotional needs of adults in the community. When they receive food, shelter, and clothing, they experience concretely God's love and concern.

10. **Flexibility:** The primary value of this skill in adult ministry is its constant acceptance of differences in adult personalities and openness to the Holy Spirit. For a program to survive, a leader must maintain flexibility and composure when responding to new and challenging situations, such as an unexpected visitor or a guest speaker who failed to show up.

11. **Tolerance:** This skill is crucial to hospitality and community building. Adult faith formation, which focuses on building a personal relationship with God, requires the visible love experience that tolerance provides.

12. **Emotional health:** Without the peace of mind that results from a constant rational response to one's own legitimate needs, a leader is less able to demonstrate any of his or her talents.

How Can These Talents Influence Adult Catechesis?

Now that you have evaluated your own talents and have seen how those skills are needed in adult faith formation ministry, you can apply this knowledge to adult catechesis.

Adults in any catechizing event represent a wide variety of God-given personalities. But adults respond more readily to and learn most easily from activities that require them to demonstrate their strongest skills. The following list provides examples of catechizing events in which adults can develop and share their leadership skills.

- Decision making by participants

- Socializing interactions (pairs, small groups, the whole group)

- Plans that participants organize in response to what they have experienced

- Ways participants can assume responsibility (refreshments, calling friends to participate)

- Questions or projects that challenge them to think logically, intuitively, or artistically

- Reflections on what others are feeling in the present group or in their day-to-day lives

- Challenges to rethink how participants have approached certain life situations before and how they will change, based on their Scripture reflections

- Opportunities for getting to know each new person in a group situation

- Analysis of which personal needs participants have not yet met

Applications to Other Parish Ministries

All ministries dealing with adults benefit from identifying the God-given talents of their volunteers and the clients who receive their services. Our aim is to allow each volunteer's personal gifts to match the needs of the ministry and its clients.

For example, volunteers who are sociable should have opportunities for interacting with people in their pastoral work. These volunteers might serve the sociable homebound grandmother who also needs human contact and dialogue. The sociable minister will spend time talking to her, instead of looking for a quick in-and-out delivery of the Eucharist or a meal. Both volunteer and client experience God's love in this fulfillment of their unique needs.

Peace Is the Most Important Talent

In conclusion, the most noteworthy principle about talents applied to adult faith formation ministry remains the importance of emotional health and its visible sign—peace. Sharing one's talents leads to enjoyment, fulfillment, lack of anxiety, and peace. Interestingly enough,

Jesus' most common phrase to the disciples and apostles after the Resurrection was "Peace be with you" (Jn 20:26). This is the gift he most wants us to have in our ministry.

The Use of Our Intellect in Visioning, Problem Solving, and Evaluation

God created your intellect to reveal the truth in so many ways: good judgment, sound wisdom, perceptiveness, knowledge, logic, intuition, artistic skill, and self-awareness. Your intellect is the primary connection between you, others, and God. Your intellect receives God's special graces of light and strength to guide you beyond your intellect's natural ability. It also helps you grow in your personal relationship with God.

So What Actually Is the Intellect?

What are the powers of the intellect all about? As Aristotle described before the time of Christ, and St. Thomas Aquinas restated by combining Aristotle's insights with Scripture in *Summa Theologica*, the intellect is the primary power of your human soul. Your soul is spirit, by nature non-material and everlasting. Your spirit or soul, made in the image and likeness of God, can reflect on itself; it is what enables you to say "I." This "I," can by its very nature see what is true, whether the question is "What is a tree?" or "Who am I?" or "Who is God?" To answer the question, you must proceed, fact by accumulated fact, to arrive at a logical conclusion about what is true. Sometimes you can also reach the truth by a simple intuition, a quick creative non-step-by-step leap. All this natural power of your spirit or soul is called intellect.

How Does Intellect Work in Ministry?

"How does intellect function?" "How can the intellect help you in your ministry?" Whenever you ask questions, you must rely on your intellect to find the answers. God made your powerful intellect to provide you with the truth. It provides you with the truth about everything. Want to know how to protect an innocent woman? Ask your intellect by asking questions. Want to know what to do with your life? Ask yourself questions. Want to know how to start an adult faith formation program in your parish? Ask questions.

To use your intellect in ministry, you need to pursue an answer to the original question, "How does intellect function?" Logical and intuitive intelligence provides the most help in adult faith formation ministry. The following descriptions and questions show how you can use logical or intuitive intelligence in ministry.

Logical Intelligence

Description: I carefully organize, in a logical form, the material I wish to cover in my teaching or other ministry work. I have confidence that my logical, step-by-step ministry planning or presentations will be accurate and powerful. I trust that my conclusions in dealing with adults or other situations are correct and are at least based on the facts of which I am aware. I choose questions that require logical, step-by-step thinking rather than just looking for rote-memory responses. I help adults to be organized and logical in their thinking, speaking, and writing. I most enjoy adults who think logically and work out problems step-by-step. I do not enjoy adults who are poorly organized, do not think clearly, and are confused or superstitious. To develop my logical intelligence, I will continue my effort to think clearly and logically. I will trust and practice my ability to arrive at the truth, step by logical step.

Questions: In what situations have I seen myself use a logical, step-by-step approach to ministry visioning, planning, problem solving, or evaluating? Do I organize my ministry planning and material on a daily, weekly, or monthly basis so that I can experience daily satisfaction in knowing where I am in achieving my ministry goals? Do I trust my God-given logical thinking in developing and carrying out my ministry activity?

Who do I know that thinks logically like myself? What other person, instead, tends to think more intuitively? Where in my ministry do I not trust my logic? Regarding current problems in my ministry, do I need to ask Jesus and Mary for assistance in logically thinking through to a solution?

Intuitive Intelligence

Description: I trust my own intuitive intelligence, believing in the insights I have in the material I prepare or the discussions I have with others. I pause and allow a person time to come up with new and intelligent solutions to a problem, showing that I trust in his or her power of intuitive intelligence. I often ask myself, "In what new way can I do this?" I look for the humor in my presentations, knowing that my intuitive, artistic intelligence can be an excellent source of humor, of the unexpected, of a new twist. I also know that humor is one of the greatest bonding tools in group process. I add a thought-provoking, open-ended creative question in my work with adults so they can share their intuitive thinking and we can enjoy the discussion. I do not enjoy people who are too conservative, unimaginative, fearful, or even too logical and orderly in their thinking. To develop my intuitive intelligence, I will keep trying new ideas and new directions. I will trust my God-given skill to come up with creative solutions to difficult problems. I will create new things in my ministry, for and with the Lord.

Questions: When did I trust my intuitive, creative intelligence to come up with a new idea, a new direction, or even a new ministry? What was the last instance in which I tried something new or creative in my ministry, whether an idea or way of presentation? What is an innovative solution that comes to mind when I try again, right at this moment, to solve a problem I am dealing with in my ministry? What adults do I enjoy sharing new ideas with because they are "new ideas" people? Where have I been successful in my creative thinking, relying on my confidence in this skill to increase its freedom to function? Where in my ministry may I need to be more open to new possibilities, as were Jesus and Mary?

How to Envision Ministry

Visioning begins the whole process of any ministry. An adult faith formation's vision begins with the pastor who perceives the value of this program for his parish. He wants to provide the adults as much formation as the children and teens receive to grow in their relationship with God. He sees the value, he sees the need, and he determines to do something about it. His plan includes hiring an adult faith formation director and helping to create an adult faith formation team and a catechists of adults team. The pastor knows that the next step involves the director and teams also envisioning an adult faith formation program.

Visioning reflects the belief that people in an organization must create or recreate a mission statement by connecting that mission to their own personal sense of purpose. That connection enhances motivation, commitment, and fulfillment. The process also deals with the reality of change in what should be the mission goals as circumstances change.

The director can lead the teams in the visioning process by following these steps:

1. Have participants write down on three-by-five-inch file cards what they see as the most important events and changes that have occurred in the world over the past five to ten years.

2. Arrange the cards on the wall in groups with titles the teams choose.

3. Then do steps 1 and 2 for the most important events and changes in the Catholic Church over the past five to ten years.

4. Do steps 1 and 2 for the most important events and changes in your parish over the past five to ten years.

5. Then discuss the trends that the team members see in relation to the cards.

6. Proceed to a recorded discussion regarding a) the purpose of the adult faith formation program, asking *"Why* are we in existence?" and b) your mission, with *"What* do we do to fulfill our purpose?" and c) your philosophy or statement of the values you hold, with *"How* do we do things here?"

7. Later, have the team review the recorded discussion (Step 6) and finalize a written summary, entitled "The Mission and Philosophy of the Adult Faith Formation Program of Our Parish."

Problem Solving and Decision Making in Ministry

The accumulation of facts regarding any problem or decision to be made in ministry provides the material on which the intellect can arrive at a solution. For example, the previous visioning process was based on the facts of events or changes. Changes in vision, making it an ongoing process, will come from new facts seen in the problem solving and decision-making situations of ministry. But how do you go about problem solving and decision making?

Both processes reflect the primary skill in the use of intellect: Ask questions to arrive at the truth. The following questions are helpful.

Problem-Solving Questions

- What is a description of the problem?

- What are the facts regarding this problem?

- Who has additional information or another perspective regarding this problem?

- What is the conflict here?

- What are some possible solutions?

- What are the potential positive and negative consequences of what seems to be the best solution or solutions?

- What are your gut feelings about the solution?

- Do you have any final thoughts?

Decision-Making Questions

- What are we trying to decide here?

- What are the facts related to this decision?

- How important is this decision?

- Does it need to be made now? If not, when?

- Who makes the final decision?

- What is at stake here?

- What additional information do we need before making this decision?

- Who else should we ask for input about this decision?

- What might be the positive and negative consequences of our decision?

- What are your gut feelings about the decision?

- Do you have any final thoughts?

Evaluation of Effectiveness in Ministry

Another use of your intellectual logic and intuition in ministry lies in evaluation. Why evaluate? You need to know the effectiveness of your ministry work. "Effectiveness" is a scary word. As a ministry leader you face your own concern, as well as the concern of others, about whether you are getting the job done. "What do they mean effective? I'm working myself to death!" Of course, what effective means in your vision of daily ministry may not be someone else's vision. Only leaders of adult faith formation can judge what is a worthwhile use of their daily ministry life, with God making the final judgment.

An example of differing visions of effectiveness occurred in a parish with a thriving Hispanic ministry. The parish had many liturgies, socials, volunteer leaders, and a large assembly. The ministry leader was justifiably proud. Then, at a parish staff meeting, a different ministry leader asked, "Since our Hispanic parish community is immersed in poverty, why are we not reaching out with social ministries to solve their real problems—lack of food and clothing, inadequate housing, and unemployment?"

Here was a challenging, broader vision. Visions can differ. Evaluation is based on one's vision. Yet the Holy Spirit can also challenge you through other people at any time as to the full effectiveness of your ministry work.

Besides relying on your vision and being open to the Holy Spirit in expanding that vision, the evaluation of effectiveness depends on challenging your intellect. When you force the intellect to evaluate by asking, "Are we getting the job done?" you can trust it to arrive at the truth. The answer will, of course, be limited by the current facts available to you.

St. John of the Cross reminded his people that God draws near to those who come together in an endeavor to know the truth. He based this on God's assertion that he would speak through Aaron and Moses when they were together for consultation (*The Ascent of Mount Carmel*, Book 2, Chap. 22, in Kavanaugh and Rodriguez, *Collected Works of St. John of the Cross*).

Other questions to ask the intellect in the evaluation of your ministry work, besides the basic "Are we getting the job done?" are the following:

- What are the facts about what we have accomplished?

- How do the facts match our vision and goals?

- Are we reaching the numbers of people that we should?

- Do we have the resources to do the job?

- Are we enjoying our work?

- Are we praying enough for our ministry?

- Who else may we need to invite as new volunteers because we need their skills?

- What obstacles may we encounter in our ministry?

- Should we reevaluate our vision?

- What would Jesus want us to accomplish in our particular ministry?

- What do others say about our ministry work that may be directed by the Holy Spirit?

Reminder: Effectiveness Comes from Talents

A final thought about the evaluation of your effectiveness is that being effective comes naturally. If you are in the right service to others, have the natural talents for it, effectiveness will just happen. It is not by magic that God's work gets done. It is not a string of supernatural miracles that God must perform for ministry to succeed. Rather, your service to others and yourself is effective when you use the talents God gave you for your ministry.

But lest you forget, the very intelligent and talented leader Saul was knocked off his horse and blinded. Taking the name Paul, he turned to a new ministry. St. Luke summarized Paul's ministry, saying that he spent his time proclaiming Jesus as the Son of God. For you also, your faith must be your primary focus in the use of your talents in ministry.

Applications to Other Parish Ministries

Visioning not only begins the whole process of ministry but needs to happen again and again, annually at the very least. And every new volunteer needs to experience being a part of the visioning process of his or her chosen ministry. This helps them determine the direction of their ministry and share the responsibility for its outcome. All it takes is a leader or companion who will, early on, draw them into a discussion of the three questions of visioning: *Why* does this ministry exist? *What* must we do to fulfill our purpose? *How* should we do things here?

Finally, every ministry requires evaluation. If you are to be effective in achieving your goals, you must welcome and rely on feedback from your volunteers and the parishioners you serve. For example, do the teens (who have the same psychology of catechesis as adults) enjoy their meetings? Are they changing their attitudes and behavior, becoming more like Jesus and Mary as a result of your catechesis with them? If not, you must create new strategies until you find what works for them.

Resolving Relationship Conflicts

Did you ever expect to see conflict between Mary and Jesus? If conflict means a difference in judgment, it most certainly happened— twice. When Jesus was twelve, he decided to stay behind in Jerusalem when the rest of the family headed back to Nazareth. It took three days for Mary to find him and when she did, she challenged his judgment (Lk 2:41–51).

Eighteen years later at the wedding in Cana, Mary challenged Jesus again (Jn 2:1–11). She told him the party was out of wine. But how was Jesus, coming from a poor family, suddenly going to produce 120 gallons of wine? There would seem to be only one solution. He had to perform a miracle. However, that would publicly show that he was the Son of God with miraculous powers. He would be forced to seriously begin his public ministry. Jesus believed that his "hour has not yet come." Mary put the ball back on Jesus' court by telling the servants to do whatever he told them. He resolved the conflict by creating the wine, possibly listening to the Holy Spirit advising him through Mary's judgment. But the conflict of judgment was real, and it began their public ministry.

Relationship conflict, the primary source of difficulties for ministry, occurs when people demonstrate their positive God-given talents. Both Mary and Jesus possessed what we call decision-making skills. Both wanted to be in charge, to say how things should be done, to have the other listen to their judgment. That is the God-given nature of decision makers. They all think they are right. Therein lies the obvious potential for conflict among the best of leaders. Whose direction will be chosen?

How Do Talents Cause Most Conflicts?

As you have seen in Mary and Jesus, natural differences among people's positive skills can cause conflict. What occurred between Mary and Jesus—a typical difference of judgment between two people with decision-making talent—remains today the most common source of conflict among leaders in ministry.

For example, if you enjoy socializing and have a lot of talent for it, and if I have very little talent for it, we may come in conflict. You like to talk a lot, and I hate it. This may become a source of friction between us. Differences in skill levels produce conflict between most talents. However, differences in skills that serve the same purpose can also create conflict. Logic and intuition are different approaches to solving problems. People conflict when one excels at and prefers solving problems logically but the other excels at and prefers solving problems intuitively.

Solutions Come When Talent Needs Are Met

The following two principles explain the importance of being able to use our God-given talents.

1. **A person with a talent has a need flowing from that talent.** Since you are human, you not only enjoy food, you need food. Similarly, possessing a skill or talent creates the need to use that skill. The twelve psychological talents each create a matching need. If you have the talent for decision making, you must act as a decision maker to satisfy that need.

2. **People enjoy fulfilling the need to demonstrate their talents, but they become angry when their talent needs are not met.** This gets at the heart of what causes conflict and how to resolve it. We identify our talents by recognizing what we enjoy doing. When we are unable to use our talents, we become angry, and anger is what primarily causes conflict among people.

Did it ever strike you that at both the temple and the wedding in Cana, Jesus showed some irritation with Mary? "Why were you searching for me? Did you not know I must be in my Father's house?" (Lk 2:49). And, "Woman, what concern is that to you and to me?" (Jn 2:4). Our basic solution to conflict lies in finding intelligent ways to meet both persons' conflicting talent needs.

One of my most enjoyable experiences of volunteer ministry was the time I spent identifying talents for more than seven hundred engaged couples. A special part of that enjoyment was seeing how well the couples came up with solutions to meeting their differing talents and differing needs. By the end of our sessions, they knew the greatest sources of future conflict and could intelligently find solutions to each other's differing needs, as much as humanly possible. One of the more humorous but typically inventive solutions was the decision by a couple to frequently go to the movies. Their reasoning was that she loved to socialize and therefore loved sitting in a crowded theatre. Though he hated to socialize, he loved sitting alone with her in the dark.

How Each Talent Causes Conflict and What to Do about It

For the best use of the following list of twelve talents, select your strongest talents from Chapter Four's "A Self-Evaluation of Your Talents"—those you rated as "Strongly" or "Occasionally." Generally, these will cause conflict for you in ministry work. For each of the following talents is a description of a) your unmet needs in a conflict, b) the other person's unmet needs, and c) recommended solutions. Read all of the following to better understand all people.

1. Decision Making

a. The conflict for me: This talent creates conflict when my need to be in charge is not met. Others do not listen to my judgment. Another difficulty for me arises when others try to tell me what to do.

b. The conflict for those with a need similar to mine: They see that I refuse to listen to their judgment. They want to be in charge. They dislike it when I tell them how to think or what to do.

c. Some solutions to the conflict: Listen to one another express your complete thinking on the issue causing conflict. Each of you should have your own area of responsibility. Insist on the principle that "the facts shall rule." Remember that you conflict because you both want your judgment to rule.

2. Sociability

a. The conflict for me: This talent creates conflict for me when I am alone. I'm not very happy when I'm not engaged in light conversation or involved in a group activity. I get angry when people shut me out of a conversation.

b. The conflict for those with a lesser need than mine: They think I talk too much. They prefer to talk about more serious matters. They feel uncomfortable, even anxious in group situations, such as team meetings and socials.

c. Some solutions to the conflict: Provide experiences for social interaction, one-to-one communication, and individual reflection. Respond to the other person's need by taking turns either talking for awhile or being quiet for awhile.

3. Organization

a. The conflict for me: I feel conflict when things are disorganized. I get irritated when other members of the team do not stick to our plan. I get angry when things are not where they should be, such as a particular schedule in a particular file.

b. The conflict for those with a lesser need than mine: They think I am too particular about details, that I waste too much time organizing things. "Live free from structure" is their motto. They enjoy operating on impulse.

c. Some solutions to the conflict: Recognize each other's different approaches to organization. Both sides need to concentrate on organizing what common sense dictates must be organized, such as a coming liturgy. As much as possible, let the naturally talented "organizer" be in charge of the organizing when it has to be done.

4. Responsibility

a. The conflict for me: I get angry when people do not get their jobs done on time. People who are not careful in what they do or say irritate me, as do those who do not think through the logical consequences of their behavior.

b. The conflict for those with a lesser need than mine: They believe I am self-righteous. They think there should be greater flexibility in getting the job done. A structured situation causes them to feel uptight.

c. Some solutions to the conflict: Efficient ministry work depends on the facts everyone accepts. Discuss a time plan based on facts, reason, and common sense for every important project.

5. Logical intelligence

a. The conflict for me: I do not understand how people can jump to a solution of an important problem without figuring it out step-by-step. People who do not know how to think things through drive me crazy. Irrational behavior always irritates me.

b. The conflict for those with a lesser need than mine: When I get so bogged down in the details, they think I am wasting their time. They wish I could relax and let the solution to a problem just suddenly float to the top.

c. Some solutions to the conflict: Accept that both logic and intuition are legitimate ways to reach the same truth, the same solution. Be understanding as the other person processes in his or her own way. (Note: Some people are strong in both logical and intuitive intelligence.)

6. Intuitive intelligence

a. The conflict for me: I hate thinking step-by-step to figure out the answer to a problem. People who dismiss my spontaneous insight or solution to a problem make me angry. People who do not trust their own quick, creative intuition irritate me.

b. The conflict for those with a lesser need than mine: They think that my quick solutions make no sense because they are "not well-thought-out." My quick solutions scare them. They challenge me to explain how I "came up with that."

c. Some solutions to the conflict: Accept that both logic and intuition are legitimate ways to reach the same truth, the same solution. Both of you must be understanding when the other person processes in a different way. (Note: Some people are strong in both logical and intuitive intelligence.)

7. Artistic intelligence

a. The conflict for me: When I am not able to express myself artistically, it depresses me. People who disrupt my enjoyment of beauty irritate me. Critics of art, music, dance, poetry, or sculpture annoy me.

b. The conflict for those with a lesser need than mine: They say with irritation that they have never really been much interested in any form of art. Hours spent on liturgical decorations are a real waste of time to them.

c. Some solutions to the conflict: Accept artistic expression as a gift that not all have. Since music, art, and dance are known mediums for God's grace, give them their respected place in liturgy and adult catechesis.

8. Counseling

a. The conflict for me: I get irritated when people are not open with me about their feelings. When I judge that they are lying about how they feel, I get angry or depressed. I become anxious when a person is good at hiding his or her true feelings.

b. The conflict for those with a lesser need than mine: Dealing with emotions is difficult for them. They do not like to be asked if they are angry, or if they love another person. They do not like to openly express any of their feelings.

c. Some solutions to the conflict: Accept each other's differences regarding the perception and sharing of feelings. Give the other more of what that person wants, which for one is more verbalization of feelings and for the other, less demand to verbalize feelings.

9. Nurturance

a. The conflict for me: I get depressed when I do not have anyone for whom to cook, clothe, house, or provide a corporal or spiritual work of mercy. When people respond coldly to my embrace, I feel badly.

b. The conflict for those with a lesser need than mine: They are irritated by physical displays of affection, like hugs, an arm around the shoulder, a touch on the arm. They feel some anger toward another person who is always trying to take care of them.

c. Some solutions to the conflict: Watch for signs that your affectionate behavior is irritating others, and accept their negative feelings about it. Be affectionate with those who are like-minded and appreciate your affection. Those who do not enjoy receiving or giving this type of affection need to accept that it is all right for you to be the way you are and for them to be the way they are.

10. Flexibility

a. The conflict for me: I hate people who are too rigid. Inflexible principles or rules with no exceptions aggravate me. Judgmental people who are not aware of all the facts make me angry.

b. The conflict for those with a lesser need than mine: They think I am too loose, maybe even immoral. They resist being flexible because it means accepting a more complicated view of life, people, and situations. They may fear life's instability; therefore, they follow a few simple principles by which to judge everything.

c. Some solutions to the conflict: Work by the principle that facts shall reign supreme. If the more flexible person can provide supporting facts, the less flexible person should agree to accept the conclusion. In other words, go by principles based on all the facts available.

11. Tolerance

a. The conflict for me: Racists anger me. People's lack of tolerance for anyone different makes me uncomfortable and irritated. I get depressed at the amount of intolerance there is, whether it is sexism, racism, or any other form of irrational intolerance.

b. The conflict for those with a lesser need than mine: They are irritated that I do not understand their feelings of fear or superiority. They are uncomfortable in the presence of those who are different, whether by gender, race, sexual orientation, or economics.

c. Some solutions to the conflict: Education and exposure to that which is feared or believed to be inferior help ensure that reason and common sense prevail.

12. Emotional health

a. The conflict for me: I am uncomfortable with those who are anxious. I have difficulty dealing with people who live under a dark cloud or appear irrational. Cowardly, greedy, or evil behavior angers me.

b. The conflict for those with a lesser need than mine: They live in an emotional world of fear, depression, and anxiety. In their minds, life is full of conflict rather than peace. They lack my long-term confidence, rationality, and peace.

c. Some solutions to the conflict: Do everything to build the self-esteem of the anxious. Reassuring them of their goodness and talents gets at the heart of their anxiety and can help give them peace. Anxious adults were children who learned they were not worthwhile. If they admit to strong anxiety, let them know as children of God that they have a right to peace and should seek counseling to eliminate their anxiety.

Other Powerful Sources of Conflict in Ministry

Other less typical, yet very powerful, sources of conflict are the weaknesses or evil that have the power to destroy ministry. These can include lying, greed, lust, jealousy, slander, and irrational or unjust control. All of these, often resulting from emotional illness or weakness, can nevertheless produce evil in their destruction of God's ministries. For example, who in parish ministry has not seen or heard first-hand the experiences of staff, volunteers, or pastors who have been lied about and driven from a successful ministry? The two virtues most needed to combat these forms of evil are reason and courage.

Despite your intelligent and courageous efforts, other forces can prevent the success of your ministry. A lack of vision or action may not be the primary obstacle. Others can choose not to support your ministry. They may include legislators on social justice issues and parishioners or staff members who, out of jealousy, racism or other irrational impulses, resist your legitimate vision and efforts. Even potential recipients of your ministry can resist your best efforts to bring them the good that God wishes for them. Each person is free to resist God's love. We are not perfect. Neither are those to whom we minister.

Applications to Other Parish Ministries

Conflict in any ministry is unavoidable because it is based on natural differences. Fortunately, almost all conflict is resolvable.

What if you walk into a meeting with your ministry volunteers and no chairs are set up? The janitor—the same one with whom you got upset yesterday over another matter—has forgotten to have them ready. You had noticed that it seemed to upset him when you described in detail how a job should be done. Since the janitor did not like to be told what to do, you decided to express your ministry needs to him in the briefest, most direct form possible. What you did was respond to this person's decision-making talent by judging from what upset him. You continue to experiment with how you relate to the janitor until both of you believe that your needs have been heard and met.

All ministries benefit in terms of peace and productivity from practicing the dictum, "Solutions come from talent needs met."

Peace Is the Result

You have just reviewed twelve other less typical causes of conflict in church ministry and human interaction. Study the descriptions and solutions well; they become a source of greater peace for your life and the lives of others. Others will look to you as a model in how you deal with conflict. Conflict resolution, God's peace, comes from a greater understanding of the truth, our differences, and our similarities.

Chapter 7

Multiplying Volunteers

Either intuition or logic provides the beginning step for recruiting most ministry volunteers. For example, a spontaneous, intuitive thought may come to you: "She would be great at hospitality in our ministry!" Or you may say to yourself in a logical manner, "We need someone to take care of hospitality at our seminar series. John is sociable and organized. Therefore, he would be great at hospitality."

Whether you rely on logic or intuition, the secret to multiplying volunteers is to first recognize that this person's talents match your ministry's needs. The second major step requires inviting that person to join you in ministry, as Jesus did with the disciples. Your invitation should include identifying how that person's specific skills are needed in your ministry. An initial interview can more specifically describe that match.

The Needs of Our Ministry

The adult faith formation program ministry has a multitude of needs. We need leaders. We need ongoing vision. We need organization and hospitality. We need an understanding of adults' needs and of how to catechize adults. We need prayer to support our work. We need a healthy spirituality that includes openness to the Holy Spirit. We need to be caring. We need to attract many volunteers. We need excellent speakers and experienced marketers. We need logic and intuitive creativity in all things. We need artistic skills and counseling skills. We need responsibility, flexibility, emotional health, and tolerance. We need the courage to achieve all the above and to counteract evil. This list can seem overwhelming, and you will identify other needs as well. Potential volunteers in your parish can bring in the skills to meet all these needs. Helpers to bring in the harvest are out there, waiting for your invitation.

How to Identify the Needed Skills in Volunteers

Church staff members, priests, and volunteers at my seminars on "Multiplying Volunteers" amaze themselves at how quickly they can identify the twelve most important skills in one another after they have filled out the "A Self-Evaluation of Your Talents" questionnaire. Having evaluated the twelve skills in yourself makes it easy to identify those same skills in another person, in a potential volunteer.

How do you spot these skills? Take for example, the skill of decision making. When you are in a discussion with a person whom you think might be a candidate for a leadership position, notice how much he or she tries to lead the conversation. He or she may even cut you off as you are talking. There is a high need being fulfilled, but it is also an example of wanting to take charge that reflects the skill you want your leader to have. A socially skilled person may take ample time to describe a simple situation to you. Common sense will dictate how to recognize each of the twelve skills from their description.

Your common sense will also help you determine if a volunteer is capable of being trained for skills in adult catechesis, public speaking, or marketing. Everyone needs levels of prayer, spirituality, openness to the Holy Spirit, and courage, but these may take longer to discern. The ministry is responsible for helping all volunteers develop these skills.

Emotional health—a sense of peace and lack of high anxiety—should be your first and primary concern in assessing the skills of every volunteer. If you have an emotionally upset or anxious personality, oftentimes spotted by irrationality in behavior, you have the greatest potential for failure in your ministry. For example, regardless of whether they are staff, volunteers, or parishioners, these individuals are more prone to dishonesty, greed, and violence. They often deal only with their own selfish needs and exhibit other destructive and harmful behaviors. You can love them and try to assist them toward health, but you must not allow them to enter ministry or stay if they are already serving as volunteers. Bishops have a major responsibility to either prevent emotionally ill candidates from entering the priesthood or to remove any emotionally ill priest from ministry until healed. In the same way, you also have the responsibility of excluding or removing the emotionally ill from volunteer work.

What Works to Attract Volunteers

The primary three steps involved in attracting volunteers are to 1) match their skills to the needs of your ministry, 2) personally call them to this ministry, and 3) follow through on your invitation. Three ways to draw in volunteers include recruiting in as many ways as possible, inviting those adults already ministered to, and praying.

1. **Match their skills to the needs of your ministry.** God gave each of us certain talents to use as our way of fulfilling God's will in our lives. We must use these talents in the ministry where they are needed. The skills people already enjoy using in other aspects of their lives, such as in their career or avocation, are natural matches to ministry.

2. **Personally call people to ministry.** There is tremendous power in the personal call to join in God's ministry. Based on adult psychology and theology, the best way to attract volunteers is to personally call people.

3. **Follow through on your invitation.** Amazingly, in ministry, this principle is often neglected. For example, many parishes offer an annual Ministry Day when members of all the ministries sit behind tables to register interested parishioners as volunteers. Yet actual personal contact between the ministry leaders and those who sign up may not happen. If it does happen, ministry leaders may fail to do a necessary follow-through to identify particular skills and to show volunteers how their talents match with the needs of the ministry. An additional caveat is that you may need to ask more than once, pointing out again which of their skills are needed in ministry. Be patient and pray. In the end, if they do not come, you will have done them a service by highlighting the skills God had given them for a different purpose.

4. **Market in as many ways as possible.** Recruiting calls for meeting the needs of your potential volunteer, which you have done by matching their talent needs to the needs of the ministry. Another major marketing principle demands multiple exposure to your message. One Ministry Day a year will not do it. To begin with, you, as one of the adult faith ministry leaders, must have volunteer recruitment on your mind daily. At every adult faith formation event, you must verbalize your volunteer recruitment invitation. Announce your specific needs and describe the particular talents you are looking for.

In all your person-to-person or group encounters, constantly keep your eyes and ears open for skills that match the various needs of your ministry. Take every opportunity to advertise in the bulletin, from the pulpit, in your adult faith formation newsletter, bulletin boards, and any events you attend where you are given a chance to talk to adults. You are proud of the ministry and you want to share the opportunity to serve.

5. **Invite adults to whom you are already ministering.** This huge opportunity, though very logical, often gets missed. You spend much effort providing an adult faith formation event, such as a seminar or group study, that draws adults interested in their adult formation, and you do not invite them to share in this ministry? If you spell out your needs and the matching skills needed, surely you will draw in one or two matches out of every twenty-five participants. Make your invitation before the break, and have a sign-up sheet for a name, phone number, and e-mail address.

6. **Depend on prayer to attract volunteers.** It is certainly true that when you match people's God-given talents to the needs of the ministry, God has already had a hand in attracting those volunteers. But if you add prayer, if you ask God for help, then much more help is present to enlighten your judgment and overcome barriers to people responding to the call. God depends on you to do your part.

Additional possibilities for attracting volunteers:

- Appeal to their baptismal responsibility to share their faith and spread God's kingdom.

- Ask them to be an instrument of God's love to others.

- Promise them training, spiritual growth experiences, and a rich community life.

- Promise to team or pair everyone in his or her ministry work.

- Provide specific task, time, and job training descriptions for each ministry need.

- Be friendly, approachable, and inviting, interacting with each person one on one.

- Provide positive witness talks given by volunteers at Mass.

- Express enthusiasm about your ministry work.

- Provide an opportunity at parish registration for sharing volunteer interests or skills.

- Offer "Come and Watch" mentoring experiences.

- Give a full-day seminar on "How to Identify Your Skills That Meet Ministry Needs."

- Provide a hospitable, warm, and exciting parish environment.

- Promise a one-year or shorter, renewable contract, flexible to their needs.

- Provide a volunteer counselor to match skills with ministry.

- Tell seniors not to bury their God-given talents at age sixty-five but to share their wisdom.

Interviews to Match Skills with Ministry Needs

You know the importance of matching skills with ministry needs. Though this can happen through informal observation of what a person says and does, the personal interview is a helpful process.

- **Skills needed by the interviewer:** Counseling is the primary skill. The most distinctive quality of this skill lies in the ability to discern how another person is feeling without that person putting it into words. Also, the counselor can accurately "read between the lines" if the client does verbalize. Other helpful qualities for the interviewer are the talents of sociability and logical and intuitive intelligence. The interview process involves drawing from the potential volunteer what their talents are and sharing the specifics of the different ministry needs.

- **Basic questions for the interviewer to ask:** What do you most enjoy doing? What have you enjoyed doing in the past? What are you really good at? What skills have others praised you for in the past? In what areas have you had training, education, or experience? What functions in ministry would best match what you enjoy doing?

A Sample Interview

INTERVIEWER   Welcome! We are going to explore together what you most enjoy doing and do well. This will reflect the specific talents or skills God has given you and how you can do God's will in your life. We will then match your skills with the specific needs for those skills in our adult faith formation work. Of course, you are probably already using those skills in your work, family life, avocation, or recreation. But our concern here is to provide you with the most enjoyable and productive fit based on your interest. Let's pray for the light and strength of the Holy Spirit to help us here. So what do you most enjoy doing now, and what did you enjoy doing in the past?

INTERVIEWEE   Without question, I most enjoy counseling. I believe I am and have been really good at it. I also enjoy being with people.

INTERVIEWER   Great, you have pinned down two strong skills: being able to counsel and being able to socialize with people. What work in adult faith formation ministry do you think requires those skills that you would enjoy doing?

INTERVIEWEE   I would most enjoy counseling volunteers, helping people discern their natural psychological skills, and matching their skills to ministry needs. I would also like to be part of a spiritual direction team that would include the need for counseling but might require further training in spiritual direction.

INTERVIEWER   Both positions need additional people. Here are those and some additional job descriptions that require both counseling and socializing skills. We also have "A Self-evaluation of Your Talents" questionnaire that you can take for further discernment of your skills. Let's pray this coming week and get back together next Thursday for a final decision.

Each job description that you provide should include a specific title accurately describing the position, the specifics about the time required, what the precise duties are, the qualifications needed, how long the commitment is, who the candidate's supervisor will be, and what training and evaluations the candidate will receive.

What Works to Retain Volunteers?

To retain volunteers, follow the same methods used to recruit them. Continue to match their skills to your ministry's needs and remind them of their personal call to ministry.

- **First principle: You continually help the volunteers assess the matching of their skills to the tasks they are performing in ministry.** The training you promised them provides the opportunity to successfully match their skills with their work. At the beginning, all training should include their personal reassessment of how they can take advantage of their unique skills for the sake of the ministry. For example, the strong decision makers can list various ways they will take charge of their area of responsibility, using the skill descriptions in Chapter Four that you have copied for them. By using the photocopied descriptions in Chapter Six that explain which situations and personalities will cause the most conflict for them, they can decide how they will personally deal with those issues.

  Following the initial reassessment of their skills for ministry, you need to praise examples you observe of their success: "I was so impressed with how well you took charge of that meeting but still gave everyone a chance to contribute!"

- **Second principle: You expand the personal relationship you began with your invitation to join the ministry.** There are so many ways to expand your personal relationship with your volunteers. Involve them in a continual visioning process regarding the ministry. Most importantly, do whatever you can to develop friendships. A simple "How are you doing?" or "How is your family doing?" lets them know of your interest in bonding with them. Simply make your time available to them. Affirm them, telling them how their ministry action touched other people. Celebrate with them by giving them birthday cards and thank-you notes. Have emergency information cards on all of them. Provide continual training opportunities and the resources, books, magazines, and videos they will need to develop their expertise. Ask for their ideas or solutions. Challenge, respect, reassure, excite, mentor, and draw them into ever-stronger bonds of family.

Applications to Other Parish Ministries

Selecting, recruiting, and retaining volunteers is the life-blood of all parish ministries interested in maintaining and expanding their services. After identifying your own ministry's special needs, you can choose among those parishioners who have skills matching your needs. You can also create new ministries that respond to unmet parish and community needs as you work at identifying and calling forth natural leaders for those new ministries. Multiplying volunteers in all ministries makes it possible to reach the needs of more and more of God's adults. Volunteers are instruments of God's love to all.

Developing a Healthy Spirituality for Adult Faith Formation

Spirituality, the growth of an adult's personal relationship with God, defines the primary purpose of both adult faith formation and adult catechesis. However, there are as many different ways to build an adult personal relationship with God as there are different human personalities. What is central to all the ways of developing spirituality? What maintains emotional health? The use of intellect, or what I call the "circle of love."

"The Circle of Love"

Jesus summarized what is central to all forms of spirituality in his three-commandments-in-one: 1) love God and 2) love our neighbor as 3) we love ourselves (Mt 22:37–39). These three elements create the "circle of love" because, in our desire to grow in our personal love relationship with God, we reach out in loving service to our neighbor. We love ourselves by using our unique God-given talents in the work we love to do.

That brings us back in the circle of love to God in loving gratitude, petitions for help, and other forms of daily, friendly conversation. We find joy, peace, and growth in our circle of love. Any authentic spirituality produces all three central elements: a personal relationship with God, loving service to others, and loving service to ourselves.

Emotionally Healthy Spirituality

The theological truths God shares with us in Scripture accurately correlate with how God made our human psychology. The story of Mary and Joseph finally finding their teenage Jesus in the Temple contains an authentic and complete summary of adolescent psychology and how all parents should handle similar situations. Here in the circle of love, with the three elements of the love commandment, we also have what produces an emotionally healthy spirituality. Those who focus their lives on a personal love relationship with God, an active service to others out of love, and an active listening to their own legitimate needs have their emotional health well under control.

To maintain emotional health, you need the following five skills:

1. The powerful use of your intellect in the spiritual aspects of life, such as in knowing God's will.

2. The ability to discern God's presence in your daily life.

3. Awareness of your own legitimate needs.

4. Courage in facing fear, suffering, evil, and other obstacles.

5. Openness to the Holy Spirit speaking to you through all members of the Body.

The Intellect Enables Us to Know God's Will

The intellect remains the most important natural human gift God has given you. Its place in spirituality, your personal relationship with

God, lies in the intellect providing the medium for that relationship. Intellect is the primary power of your soul, of your person. You primarily communicate with other people, and they with you, through the intellect. You talk to God by means of your intellect. In turn, God communicates to you through the graces of light and strength given to your intellect.

You will, however, personally and psychologically experience God's activity only as your own intellect functioning. God will not communicate to you through voices. God is constantly present with you, hearing directly everything you say or think as you converse with God. All you hear in return is your own thinking, your own intellect. People will say they hear God responding, answering their questions, but that return conversation from God is their own imagination, directed by their own thinking or feelings. It is not God's voice. It requires reason and discernment to understand God's wisdom coming to you.

If your intellect is the medium for your relationship and conversation with God, how can it help you? The intellect helps you to know God's will for your life. "God's will" includes knowing:

- what work you should spend your life doing

- whom you should marry and befriend

- what is right and wrong for your moral life

- all the other details of your life

All of these decisions represent what you need to live life well so that God will say at the end of your life, "Well done, good and trustworthy [servant]" (Mt 25:21).

At the heart of all four "God's will" categories lies the fundamental principle that God expects you to use your intellect to make decisions. God does not want you to wait for an answer. For example, St. John of the Cross, one of the greatest doctors of spirituality of the church, presents a lengthy case that God no longer speaks to people as he had done before the time of Christ. John of the Cross states that God "is ever desirous that insofar as possible people take advantage of their own reasoning powers. All matters must be regulated by reason save those of faith" (*The Ascent of Mount Carmel,* Book 2, Chap. 22, para. 13, in Kavanaugh and Rodriguez, *Collected Works of St. John of the Cross*).

How to Figure Out by Reason
All Four of the "God's Will" Categories

1. How do you find out what work God wants you to spend your life doing?

From your intellect, you reason that God made you in such a way that you enjoy using the talents God gave you. Your intellect then concludes that, if you do the work in your life that you enjoy and do well, that is, use the specific talents God gave you, God's will gets done.

2. How do you know whom God wants you to marry and befriend?

From observation and experience, you conclude that compatibility of personality makes for enjoyable marriages and enjoyable friendships, which a loving God certainly wants for you. Compatibility comes from matching God-given talents. In fact, all twelve of the talents described in Chapter 4 produce compatibility. When people are reasonably similar in all talents, except for decision making, they will enjoy the same ways of doing things and thus reduce the potential for anger and suffering in their relationship.

As for decision making, two high-control persons will not work well together. Nor will two people who do not enjoy making decisions. On the other hand, if one of two people likes to be in charge while the other likes to have someone else in charge, their relationship will thrive.

God's will for our happiness gets done without the need for only one possible pre-ordained match.

3. How do you know what is right and wrong for your moral life?

You must rely on your faith and the sources that convey God's truth. God provided Scripture and established the church to guide your thinking and sense of morality. Over the years, theologians like St. Thomas Aquinas (*Summa Theologica*) have approached the Scripture with human intellect to logically figure out how God expects one to act. God expects you to use your own informed reason to determine right from wrong.

4. How do you know God's will for all the other details of your life?

Refer again to St. John of the Cross' statement that God "is ever desirous that insofar as possible people take advantage of their own reasoning powers. All matters must be regulated by reason save those of faith." You must experience quite a sense of freedom to know how much God expects you to use your own intelligence in the details and decisions of your life.

The Intellect Controls Our Imagination

Another great doctor of spirituality, St. Teresa of Avila, considered control of the imagination the greatest contribution to spiritual life. She constantly warns her sisters of the danger of the imagination and the need to discern its difference from the functioning of the intellect. The imagination "flies about quickly" but it is not the intellect, she said. She described how her intellect kept her focused in prayer and deepened her relationship with God while her imagination distracted her. Both

Teresa and John of the Cross advised that one should be wary of "visions and voices." Normally such experiences are due to the imagination. Teresa said to "resist them always" (*The Interior Castle*, VI:3, in Kavanaugh and Rodriguez, *Collected Works of St. Teresa of Avila*).

This may remind you of the irrational and non-theological advice to wait for God's voice to tell you what to do, including in ministry decisions. However, in all ministry decisions, collect the facts and make intelligent judgments that are logically based upon those facts. This is how God's will gets done, as long as you also continually pray for God's light and strength.

The Presence of God in Daily Life

An awareness of how God works in your life is an element of healthy spirituality. It grounds you in the reality of God's presence at all times. How do you become aware of God's power in your daily life? You need spiritual direction. You need to find a companion to encourage you to share your stories of how you experience God working in your life. That companion will ask you simple questions to get you started, such as "Where has God been in your life this past week?" or "As there is a God-given component in all human experience, tell me about some significant event in your life recently." Your companion sits back and lets you tell your story. He or she trusts that you will discover for yourself how God is working in your life, reflecting only at times on what you have said, giving no evaluations or interpretations. Both of you will finish in wonder at how much insight the Holy Spirit provided in your attempt to explore God's presence in your life.

Circle of Love: As You Love Yourself

You need to listen to your own legitimate needs. Listening to your needs and responding to them represents the primary principle for emotional health. Only you and God truly know what your needs are because God made you unique. Others can know your needs, but only if you express them. You are responsible for meeting your own needs, just as you are responsible for helping to meet the needs of others.

A person knows when he or she is working in the wrong line of ministry. When someone who loves to socialize is hidden in a cubicle, typing during all hours of volunteer ministry, that special talent remains hidden. God wants you to use the talents you know you possess. Only you have the power to discern your need and to act upon it. God trusts the intelligence given to you to decide what is wrong and how to change the situation.

God loves you in the gift of talents. You love yourself by using the talents that give you joy. You love others and they love you through the service of sharing your talents out of your personal love for God. This "circle of love" transcends time.

What about the needs of others when they conflict with your needs? Just as you use your intellect to discern your own needs, you must also discern the legitimacy of your needs in the face of others. Having a very sick child can mean staying up all night in spite of your desperate need for sleep, but the legitimacy is obvious. In any situation of conflicting needs, trust your intelligent judgment to come up with a reasoned choice. Often, reasonable alternatives are available, such as a spouse or friend who can help care for the sick child.

Courage against Fear, Suffering, and Evil

Who can deny the effect of fear-driven procrastination on the success of ministry? The evil of dishonesty that is borne out of jealousy? The conflict that prompts the firing of an effective ministry leader? Of all the solutions to ministry problems, courage offers the most hope. Courage attacks the primary sources of ministry problems: fear, suffering, and evil.

Courage is the strength to do what you know should be done. It begins with discernment. You pray to understand what should be done and to be given the strength to do it. St. Paul defined courage when he said, "Suffering produces endurance [courage], and endurance produces character, and character produces hope, and hope does not disappoint us, because God's love has been poured into our hearts through the Holy Spirit that has been given to us" (Romans 5:3–5).

Consider now how courage can deal with each of the three major sources of ministry problems.

1. **Courage against fear:** Procrastination normally represents the presence of fear: "I put off this ministry task because of my fear I will not do it well." Often unheard consciously, this little voice must be challenged by your courage. Start by asking yourself or the group: "Are we afraid we will not do this well?" The answer will easily come.

   Suppose the reply is that you are afraid. The next question to ask in establishing the truth of your goal or vision is, "Why do we want to do this work?" This will lead to the next question, "What must we do to get the job done?" Getting the job done will involve a series of small steps toward achieving your goal. For example, "I will write a chapter a week" works better than "I will write a book."

   To demonstrate your skills in the face of fear, remember the passage "Whatever you ask for in prayer, believe that you have received it, and it will be yours" (Mk 11:24). This reflects the psychological fact that regular, concrete imagining of the final success of a project enables you to accomplish the task. Star athletes use this technique. So can you in God's ministry.

2. **Courage against suffering:** Our loving God does not want you to suffer but the laws of physics, combined with driver inattention, produce a great deal of suffering in auto accidents. That is why you intelligently try to avoid suffering by driving carefully. When suffering becomes unavoidable, recall that God can bring good out of all suffering. Therefore, pray daily for courage. Offer the suffering to God for the sake of the good that God can give to others because of your conscious acceptance.

Understand that in a particular instance you may need to meet the needs of someone else, even though this stands contrary to your needs and it will cause suffering.

3. **Courage against evil:** The definition of evil in ministry is this: the intention of one person to do another person harm. Jesus in the garden of Gethsemane provides an excellent model for dealing with evil in ministry. The Sanhedrin leaders intentionally sought to do him harm. Often, the person intending the evil may be emotionally ill.

A great concern for ministry is the power of dishonesty. Any leader in conflict with another may lie about the other person's behavior, intending to undermine his or her reputation with other leaders. Courage, on the part of the offended, requires speaking up with the facts in his or her favor, preferably in writing. Because the offended often do not know of the lie, the leaders must courageously seek out the facts from the person accused when they are told negative statements that could seriously affect attitudes or decisions involving the accused.

Applications to Other Parish Ministries

Spirituality must function at the heart of every ministry. All is lost if ministry involves only external services, such as St. Vincent de Paul food drives, catechumenate lectures, children's catechesis that focuses only on rote learning, or small faith communities that are nothing more than social time and theological debate.

The volunteers and the adults who are serviced must grow in spirituality, in their personal relationship with God. City, county, and state services can provide for most physical, emotional, and educational needs. Although church ministries may provide similar services, they are primarily responsible for drawing both volunteers and clients into a growing love relationship with God and with each other.

The Spirit Speaks Through Everyone

Spirituality as applied to your ministry also requires that you practice listening to the Holy Spirit who speaks through all the members of the church, St. Paul's mystical Body of Christ. John of the Cross tells us that God chooses not to speak to us directly as God had done in the Old Testament. Rather, he insists that God intends us to listen to our own intelligence, which would include studying what God has told us in Scripture and tradition. John of the Cross however, insists that the Holy Spirit will also speak to us through the thoughts and judgments of others (*The Ascent of the Cross,* Book 2, chap. 22, in Kavanaugh and Rodriguez, *Collected Works of St. John of the Cross*). This certainly applies to your ministry work. As a leader, search out everyone's input to see where reason would suggest the Spirit wants to go.

At Cana, the Spirit spoke to Jesus through his mother to tell him to perform the miracle, in spite of his reluctance. Likewise, you need to be alert to what others say. It is necessary to make the final judgment on what others share with you, but you must remember that God may be speaking through what they share.

Chapter 9

Service and Building Community

On a hot summer morning while walking to an early Mass, I met an elderly "bag lady." Her clothes were stained, her white hair uncombed. Her large, clear plastic bag seemed to contain all her belongings. She asked me how far ahead it was to the next town and was relieved when I told her it was just a few blocks. I asked if she had any water and she said, "No." I offered her the twenty-ounce bottle of water I was carrying. Her first reaction was concern for me being without water. I told her I could get another one at the nearby store. She graciously accepted the bottle and continued on with her broken gait.

Five minutes later, as I continued my walking, I passed a bus stop shelter with a bench on which slept a seemingly homeless middle-aged man. An old bicycle was tucked in against the end of the bench. I considered leaving some money with him; instead I just continued on to church. At Mass I thought, "I should have given it; he will be gone by the time I walk home." After Mass, he still lay there sleeping. This time I checked my wallet. I had a twenty, a ten, a five and some ones. I started to put the twenty dollars in his curled-up hand, but then I thought maybe I should leave a ten instead. Finally I decided to give him the twenty. As I walked away it occurred to me, "This is my brother. Of course I had to give the twenty." I later reflected that I never even considered making it thirty.

I had never noticed marginalized people in this area of the city before, but of course they are everywhere. The most significant behaviors of Jesus included his active service to the poor, sick, despised, and other marginalized people who needed help. God wants us to copy Jesus' love. Imitating his love for the marginalized represents an obvious part of church ministry and the life of every Christian. Nevertheless, a review of modern Catholic literature on ministry and spirituality often shows little interest in this "how to love your neighbor" expression of our faith. One must go to books on social justice to find the concern. However, what is actually happening in parishes and in individual lives in reaching out to the marginalized raises hope for the future of all God's family.

We Are Family

The key to service and building community is the question of family. "How can we nurture the family of God?" The more we believe that this is family, that all these other people are actually my sisters and brothers, the more ready we are to bring about the kingdom of God in this world. As family, we exercise real concern for the needs of all the rest of the family. These needs include hunger, homelessness, unemployment, sickness, bigotry, and other ills that should not be happening to our sisters and brothers. Service reflects concern for family. Building community is also a question of family. In fact, to build great community in the parish we only need to keep in mind the question "What would we do for family?" This is the guiding principle that will easily produce many powerful ways for change.

What is the theology of family and, therefore, of service? Our Father made us in the image and likeness of God, the Trinity. The Holy Spirit is pure love, the result of the love of the Father for the Son. The personal love relationships of family reflect being made in the likeness of that Trinity. We will be together, all of God's family, for all eternity. Jesus reminds us that what we do for the least we do for him, who is God. Not to have done everything we can for our sisters and brothers in this life, with whom we will be together forever, is a fearful thought. Love of God and love of our sisters and brothers should always motivate our service.

How Does Service Catechize Adults?

Catechesis brings adults into a growing personal relationship with God that expresses itself in service. Yet the very act of service seems to produce growth in a love relationship all by itself. In their document *Our Hearts Were Burning Within Us*, the U.S. bishops affirm this happening, as do, for example, diocesan social justice directors. The question remains, "Why?"

On a typical weekday afternoon, inside the Andre House food service building, twenty volunteers from local churches meet each other for the first time and loudly labor, cutting up lettuce, carrots, tomatoes, and cucumbers for salad. Others prepare spaghetti and sauce. Throughout the large kitchen, the sound of cheerful chatter echoes as they work. Tables and chairs are set up outside to handle the seven hundred homeless and other poor who will come through the lines. With joyful faces, the kitchen crew become servants dispensing food onto the paper plates of those passing through. They love every minute of serving and talking to the guests, and they rejoice in their hearts and minds.

What is going on? The volunteers are being catechized. They experience taking part in God's tremendous love for the supposed least of our brethren. They contribute their own loving service to make God's love happen. The "cheerful chatter" in the kitchen reveals what group after group discovers. They build relationships with many new people in the space of an afternoon. They experience firsthand what the universe is really all about. God is love, and together we are caught up in the richness of the love that God wants for our family.

Who Needs Service?

If you look for needs, you find the need for service. Does your particular family have needs? You serve those needs. Does your work environment have needs? This is a major area where you can provide service with your unique talents. Does your church community have needs? Volunteering is needed. Does the wider community, including the world, have needs? They, too, are your sisters and brothers.

The adult faith formation program director and teams need to envision what the family, work, church, and wider community need. This visioning includes developing a service from scratch.

A Case Study: Starting a Hispanic Ministry

When I started an adult faith formation program a few years ago, I first challenged the governing team to examine the U.S. census report obtained from the city planner. The planner had provided data for each two-square block area within the parish boundaries. Categories of the census included race, age, income, level of education, living conditions (for example with, plumbing or none), household types and expenses, disabilities, language spoken at home, occupation, and many other items.

In the search to identify the parish community's unmet needs, the governing team was surprised by the high number of Hispanics that lived within the parish boundaries. Though traditionally Catholic, only about forty of the 2,500 Hispanics attended Sunday Mass. There are also 2,500 Anglos in the parish. Two-thirds of the Hispanics listed Spanish as the language spoken at home. The language of the home is the language of the heart, the language of one's personal love relationship with God. So the team had their work cut out for them.

Armed with the statistics, the Anglo adult faith formation director and a bilingual Hispanic team member presented a three-night seminar, in Spanish and English, based on one of the bishops' documents on the Hispanic presence in the U.S. church. Nineteen Hispanics and three Anglos attended and agreed to form a Hispanic ministry for the parish, with the pastor's verbal and financial support. A follow-up weekly training series in leadership skills taught the Hispanic ministry team how to develop their own plans and action. They took charge and have stayed in charge ever since, leading a Sunday Spanish Mass and other activities, which are also attended by Anglos.

This Hispanic ministry example presents us with some conclusions about service:

- You have to assess the real needs of the parish and the world around you.

- From among those needs for service, you must judge which are most important and how much you can reasonably accomplish.

- You must have the courage to develop new services where needed.

- Both parish staff and volunteers need to understand that only a real dependence on trained and self-sustaining volunteer leadership can provide the many needed services for God's family.

What Services Should a Parish Have?

Most parishes already offer pastoral care for the sick, homebound, and aged, and, in addition, funeral hospitality. Every parish, though, needs to involve itself directly in helping all the marginalized, whether

due to race, poverty, addiction, or emotional illness, as Jesus did. The
St. Vincent de Paul Society usually provides at least food, clothing,
rent, and gas money for walk-ins. Reaching out to others in need by
marketing parish human services could provide service opportunities
for so many more parishioners. Do they have to be Catholic? No,
the whole community is family. In many parishes, running an
"upward bound" job bank that depends on the cooperation of
employer-parishioners would meet a serious need. This service not
only helps the poor find jobs but also serves those living from
paycheck to paycheck. Ministry to those in prison and parish
counseling services for families provide additional service opportunities
for parishioners.

Legislative committees should be established in as many parishes
as possible, consisting especially of parishioner lawyers and even a
legislator or two. Bound together by a diocesan-wide network, these
committees could focus on bringing about justice for the marginalized,
whether in matters of health, job training, equal pay, sexism, or other
issues. They could address justice issues regarding women in the work
force or in church ministry. They could also pursue city, county, and
state legislative changes or additions.

The legislative committee relies on the potential of volunteer
leadership in meeting the need for wide-ranging services. If doctors
and lawyers can set aside a few hours a week to do *pro bono* work for the
poor, could other parishioners find a way to offer their own unique
talents for those in need? You must call your parishioners to service.

Building Community on the Family Model

The primary and easy way for the adult faith formation program to
help build parish community lies in seeing the family as a model for
action.

Begin by asking the question, "What should a family do?" You can
list many characteristics, but here are a few to start:

- Love one another.

- Take care of the necessities of life for one another.

- Pray and worship together.

- Take on and raise new members.

- Have fun together.

The second question becomes, "How do we build a community modeled after family?" The characteristics of being a family correspond with the following community-building actions:

1. **Love one another.** The observation of how the early church community loved one another demonstrates how to build community. The observers might have been referring to an attitude of love the Christians had toward one another. But they might also have seen behaviors that strengthened their love, such as how they shared so that no one went without.

   A loving and sincerely friendly attitude needs active development. Experiment with this principle and discover that attitude is learn able. Another major help involves your choice of volunteers for the hospitality ministry. They must be highly sociable and warm, thus able to model a loving attitude for everyone.

2. **Take care of the necessities of life for one another.** Actions speak louder than words. Your behavior toward those in need of food, clothes, shelter, and employment naturally follows from your love of your sisters and brothers. This service catechizes, but service also builds community.

3. **Pray and worship together.** If you have attended a great
liturgy, you know the power of community. It takes talented
musicians, a priest with natural drama and speaking skills, a
sermon that deeply connects Scripture with your daily life
and, of course, a community of loving, friendly people who
join in the singing, responses, and welcoming of others
before, during, and after Mass. Like a family gathered around
a Thanksgiving meal, the sense of unity at Mass builds
community.

4. **Take on and raise new members.** The Rite of Christian
Initiation of Adults, which takes on those who aspire to
become Catholic, presents an extraordinary model for
building community. On the journey of faith, each candidate
receives a companion from the parish. They share with each
other and the whole group as they explore their relationship
with Jesus. Emotional support produces family-like bonds.
They not only learn together, they pray and spend quality
time together during liturgy events. The community-building
power of this process can give you new ideas for what will
work in building the total parish community.

5. **Have fun together.** Were you ever tempted to believe the
parish festival was only about raising money? It builds
community. Is serving donuts after Mass worth it? When
two hundred people sit down and chat over donuts and
coffee or juice on a Sunday, you are building community.
The St. Patrick's Day dance builds community. Having fun
together represents a powerful binding force for individual
families and your church community.

The list of ways to build community, based on the model
of family, is endless. Additional characteristics of family could
include concern for one another, sharing feelings, listening to
one anothers' needs and stories, consoling, forgiving, being
positive toward one another, gathering together at mealtime,
and visiting relatives and friends. All these build church

community. So have fun with the family model as you plan your future action. This model provides you with the number one criterion for building community.

Applications to Other Ministries

Your ministry may have its own natural opportunities for service, like pastoral care or St. Vincent de Paul. Many other ministries can also involve their volunteers and clients in wider service outreach, whether it be in liturgy, teen ministry, children's catechesis, the parish school, small faith communities, or Knights of Columbus. Service to others in need remains the expected expression of all catechized adults.

Within service, of course, all ministries need to advocate loving service to one another's needs within their own group of volunteers and within their families at home.

Marketing

Do you want your parish's adult faith formation program to serve large numbers? First establish a prayer group to support your ministry, and then, market. Marketing means launching an aggressive campaign to bring more and more adults into a growing personal relationship with God. God wants numbers. God's concern embraces all sons and daughters, not just a select few.

We bear a major burden of responsibility as God's ministers to find "what works" in bringing people to our events. Without question, much of that burden rests on the quality and effectiveness of the events themselves. Just getting the parishioners to us is also a major challenge.

Before dealing with what works in drawing people to the service of our ministry, we need to discuss the difficulty some in church ministry have with the word "marketing." At full-day seminars on marketing for church staffs, I typically encounter the discomfort this word creates for God's ministers. So the participants and I begin with an open discussion of potential theological or spiritual principles that might support a marketing mentality in our ministry endeavors. For example, Thomas Aquinas' dictum that grace builds on nature supports using what naturally works in attracting people to religious experiences. Pepsi-Cola has developed the science, based on how God created the human personality, to get people to buy their product. Why should we not use such insights to entice people to the greatest product of their lives: their personal relationship with God?

All you need to pray for is light, strength, and the courage that produces perseverance. Here are the seven action steps or principles for marketing within the parish:

    1. Search out parishioners' real needs and design your marketing strategy to meet those needs.

2. Have the staff, pastor, and other priests participate in the marketing program.

3. Develop a subcommittee of parishioner-experts in sales and marketing.

4. Market in different ways, as many people may not respond until you have contacted them five times or more.

5. Multiply the person-to-person contacts in inviting adults to participate.

6. Market when you already have adults present at church.

7. Set your goals and remain firmly convinced greater and greater numbers will come.

Marketing to Real Needs

Searching out parishioners' needs and designing your marketing to meet those specific needs demands major work. Yet responding to real needs reflects the primary principle of all the best contemporary books on marketing and sales. If your parish adults respond more readily to Bible study as a way to grow closer to God, provide Bible study.

What are "felt needs"? These are needs that reflect adults' own perceptions of what they need. You may have your own judgments as to their needs, but until people tell you themselves, you risk making errors in marketing. Even so, you can make mistakes if you do not ask them the right questions, including time and cost questions, under the right conditions. Interviews or questionnaires, either given in group or person-to-person sessions, are useful strategies for assessing parishioners' needs.

Ask the right questions.

Preface your questions with the purpose of the adult faith formation program, which is to deepen parishioners' personal relationship with God. For example, start with, "To deepen your personal relationship with God, which of the following services would be most helpful to you?" Then, list the following:

- seminars on specific areas of interest

- group studies

- outreach services

- group or individual spiritual direction

- small faith groups

- the parish library with individual home study assistance

- retreats

- counseling

- group prayer and liturgy opportunities

- other_____

The "right" questions are those that reflect your awareness that today's U.S. Christian adults expect both spiritual and practical services. They unconsciously understand the primary principle of adult catechesis: You are catechized by putting your faith into practice. They want light on the important moral issues of the day, including work ethics. They want to learn how to serve others better and be better parents and friends. They want to deepen their relationship with God through their day-to-day lives.

Your questions must also target single adults, who comprise more than half of the adult population. If these Catholics are not attending church, you need to provide programs to attract them.

Ask time and cost questions.

Time and cost questions deal with what adults feel will make it possible for them to take part in the events of the program. Therefore, needs-assessment questions include whether they prefer to work during evenings, afternoons, mornings, weekdays, Saturday half-day or full-day, Sunday connected to the morning Mass, or Sunday afternoon or evening sessions.

Cost questions may not be necessary if your parish's policy is not to charge for seminars. Some parishes find that charging for events, such as seminars, can dramatically increase attendance. Parishioners motivated to attend may think, "If I paid for this, it must be worthwhile," or "Because I paid for it I have to go, and I should attend all the sessions." In your questions, you can include a range of possible fees (0, $5, $10, $15, $20, or___?) for a three-session seminar as a baseline, stating that the purpose is to help support the new program offerings.

Ask questions under the right conditions.

The conditions under which you carry out your needs assessment will also influence the accuracy of the results. A typically good time for a group assessment is right after the sermon during or right before Sunday Mass, following an introduction by the pastor or the adult faith formation director. Then provide parishioners with two-sided questionnaires, printed on colorful letter-size card stock. Have golf pencils ready in the pews and instruct parishioners to place the completed questionnaires in the regular offering basket during collection. Having the parishioners take the questionnaires home to return the following week does not work, nor does mailing the questionnaires.

You can expect at least a 10 percent return using the Mass approach and only 1 percent using home mailing. You can also use a "telemarketing" approach to derive as much as a 33 percent response.

Pastor and Staff Marketing

The pastor commands the greatest strength for motivating parishioners to attend any program. Starting up an adult faith formation program requires the pastor's aggressive support from the pulpit and his active participation in the program. The pastor's involvement might include presenting seminars of his own choice (even if it is only one a season) and his presence at others (even if only to give an introduction). Other opportunities are found in events, such as monthly sessions called "The Pastor's Coffee and Questions." Easily drawing fifty or more parishioners, these sessions are opportunities for the pastor to respond to parishioners' questions on theology. For example, at one parish, a session is held monthly after an 8:30 A.M. weekday Mass. It includes a free light breakfast served to the primarily senior citizen participants. Many pastors are surprised at how comfortable these informal sessions are and at the powerful relationships they build.

Once again, the director must maintain constant communication with the pastor as to how the vision is unfolding in the marketing successes and difficulties. A quarterly written report to the pastor reflects the director's challenge to make things continually happen as well as supports the value of the program. One monetary principle regarding value is that the more services you provide, the more dollars will show up in the collection basket, enabling you to provide more services.

Staff support for the adult faith formation program can produce immediate results in numbers due to the contacts they already have with so many adults in the parish. For example, the religious education director in an average-sized parish may have more than one hundred adult catechists and more than one thousand parents connected to his or her religious education program. Marketing includes providing services to staff members, including a day or evening of recollection for the religious education volunteers. You can also offer trained staff the opportunity to conduct their own seminars within the adult faith formation program that will attract their adult contacts.

The Marketing Subcommittee of Experts

Without question, a marketing subcommittee of volunteer parishioner experts in marketing and sales provides your best natural hope for success. Such experts exist in every parish. The pastor and staff can suggest parishioners who might qualify and seem interested in the needs of the parish. Just one of these on the adult faith formation team can assume responsibility for creating the subcommittee to provide the team with in-house training and wisdom in marketing.

Market Many Different Ways

Positive response to marketing can take five or more different presentations of your product or service. Thus, the more varied ways and times you contact parishioners, the better chances they will respond. Parishioners can be contacted in person, in print, or by phone. Marketing opportunities include announcements made by the priest or reader before or after Mass, sermonettes about the program during Mass, short "pitches" at all seminars or other adult faith formation events, presentations at other ministry meetings, and one-to-one conversations after Mass.

Printed marketing requires a seasonal brochure of offerings, with fall and spring editions at a minimum. These slick-stock brochures should reflect professional and attractive design and color, along with well-thought-out and presented copy. Be sure to include the pastor's introductory paragraphs describing the vision of the adult faith formation program. Spend the money to have the first edition done by a professional copy design and printing firm, and then just change the copy and color for each subsequent issue. Also produce a weekly bulletin section on upcoming adult faith formation events and reviews of past events that were successful. Sunday bulletins and every event should include well-designed flyers for each forthcoming seminar, with a registration form at the bottom to detach and mail in or drop off at the office. Other possibilities include: posters in and around the parish buildings; racks for the program brochure; the latest copies of past sermons; and issues of the *Catholic Update* series. For more exposure, publish a quarterly newsletter that includes detailed information on adult faith formation activities, reflections by the director, team members, and parishioners, and a series of volunteer job descriptions.

Phone marketing or telemarketing in the United States has become a major marketing tool for good reason. Whereas marketing by mail only receives a 1 percent return, professional telemarketing almost always produces sales in one out of every three calls. This reality suggests that you should experiment with providing volunteers with tactfully worded scripts that invite parishioners to program events. Reputable telemarketing firms strongly rely on an honest belief in the value of their product and simply present that to the consumer, trusting in the power of personal relationship.

A primary principle of marketing is that you should constantly experiment with new ways to see what works best.

Multiply Person-to-person Contacts

Personal invitation remains the most powerful of marketing tools. Theological reflection reminds us of the astounding reality that the Holy Spirit speaks to others through us. In this case, you are inviting adults to grow in personal relationship with God. How can you go wrong if you invite them to your program offerings every time? So invite, invite, and invite. Outside before and after Mass, before and after all your program events, in all reasonable places and times, describe the value of the latest offerings to parishioners, and personally invite them to join you.

What does multiplying contacts mean? Multiplying contacts refers to encouraging others to join you in inviting others. By urging everyone to invite others, you mathematically multiply your efforts. The apostles spread the good news rapidly with this same process. This can start with your teams and spread out to all your other volunteers and beyond. Every adult faith formation event can produce a new set of multiplying apostles excited about the program and commissioned to spread the word of invitation.

Market Where Adults Are Already Present

You already have the numbers. So many adults ready for your adult faith formation services have arrived on the church premises. Where are they? As mentioned earlier, a religious education program can have more than one hundred catechists and one thousand parents involved at church. The catechists are hungry for personally growing in their faith and relationship with God. Each week, parents who bring their children to catechism may potentially accept the need to grow in their personal relationship with God. Catechumenate leaders need help in their presentations to catechumens and their sponsors each week. The many services and social organizations of the parish would love another speaker. Events proceeding or following daily and Sunday Masses can draw in those already at church. Retired seniors especially respond to offerings connected to breakfast after daily morning Mass.

Applications to Other Parish Ministries

No ministry should look down on marketing. Marketing has its roots in our Catholic theology and spirituality. Because God invites all people into a love relationship, numbers do count. However, people have other preoccupations demanding their time and energy. Therefore, they need to be "sold" or they need to "buy into" a growing personal relationship with God.

Every parish ministry needs to draw, through marketing and prayer, more and more people as volunteers or clients to their services, whether it be adult faith formation, liturgy, or adult or children's catechesis. Why not use the techniques of attracting people that modern marketing has found to work?

Greater Numbers Will Come

If you set your goals high and remain firmly convinced that greater and greater numbers will come, it will happen. If you have accurately assessed the felt needs of your people, and you keep trying many ways and many times to fulfill those needs, success begins to multiply. Why should it not succeed for your adult faith formation program? You have the most that the world or existence has to offer. What need of adults is deeper in their being than that of a growing personal love relationship with their Creator and with one another as loving daughters and sons in God's family? The quality and accuracy of your program in meeting those needs can always be improved. Your strategies for successfully marketing that program can always be improved. But once again, what you need most is hope and courage.

Where Does the Program Fit in the Parish?

This "where does it fit?" question may represent the most perplexing of problems facing the adult faith formation program. Tackle this question with 1) a description of what the adult faith formation program can do in the parish; 2) a description of what the program can do for other ministries; 3) a description of what the program cannot do; 4) some possible organizational applications; and 5) a description of what remains the hope for the future of the program in the parish.

What the Program Can Do

Without question, adult catechesis represents the primary service of this program. Whether in seminars, study groups, prayer experiences, service outreach, community building, or volunteer development, this program catechizes adults. It provides as many opportunities for growth in adults' personal love relationship with God and with each other as can be developed. You must possess a deep understanding of adult psychology and adult religious experience for the sake of helping people achieve that relationship. Whether adults grow by knowledge of God or the application of God to everyday living, you humbly search how to unite adults with one another in a family united to God.

What the Program Can Do for Other Parish Ministries

The main contribution of this program to other ministries flows from its primary skill in adult catechesis. The director, the adult faith formation governing team, and the catechists of adults team all provide consultation on request in dealing with adults connected with other ministries. For example, if other ministries request adult catechesis for their adult volunteers or the participants in their own ministries, the director and team members should always be available. Liturgy development based on sound tenets of adult catechesis will always benefit the program. Opportunities for liturgy development vary from seminars, workshops, and retreats to individual spiritual direction and counseling by those trained in such skills.

What the Program Cannot Do

Although you deeply desire to assist all adults in the parish to develop their love relationship with God and with each other, the program remains human. Limitations of time and skills represent part of that human limitation. The ideal is for an adult faith formation director to develop the governing team and the catechists of adults team into powerful self-functioning entities that market, administrate, and provide catechesis to the entire adult parish. The U.S. bishops instruct every adult faith formation program to catechize all parish adults. That demands the full commitment of time, energy, and skills of the adult faith formation program director and teams.

Possible Organizational Applications

Each parish must develop its own applications in its overall manner of dealing with adults. It may be more feasible for a parish to assign a catechist, the director of children's catechesis, or a volunteer director working under another staff person, as the temporary "director" of adult faith formation, in order to get the program functioning. Funding for a full-time director should follow, helping to make adult faith formation a parish priority.

"Turf" issues can also arise between ministries over who is to offer service to adults. The central dynamic is that turf issues typically involve two or more personalities who have decision-making talents. Each trusts his or her own judgment and wants to be in charge. To resolve turf issues, have a rational discussion of what makes the most sense in dividing up areas of responsibility.

Another caveat reflects the obvious need for the other parish ministries to maintain their own volunteer groups. Even though the adult faith formation program has a major concern for attracting and developing adult volunteers as an important part of adult catechesis, this should remain only as a consulting and enrichment seminar service offered to the other ministries.

What Hope Shines in the Future?

The U.S. bishops hope for a lot. They want an adult faith formation program in every parish. They want all adults catechized, provided with full opportunities to grow in their personal love relationship with God. The hope that shines reflects the glory of all adult parishioners involved in loving service at home, church, work, and the world. Worship in community will reverberate with such richness. Justice to all will elevate our human existence. God's kingdom will come.

First Year Timeline

This suggested timeline for starting an adult faith formation program refers to the pages in this book that deal with each stage of the process. **After the pastor chooses an adult faith formation director (11), the adult faith formation director begins to plan the program:**

First Two Weeks (July 1-14)

1. Director meets with pastor to share and develop a mutual vision of the adult faith formation program for this parish (13).

2. Director meets individually with all parish staff members to ask for their vision of the parish needs for adult faith formation, what they are already doing in this area, and how they might like to contribute (12).

First and Second Months (July-August)

3. The director selects members of the adult faith formation team, with the assistance of the pastor and staff, and develops a team vision for the program. The director discusses budget projections with the pastor and business administrator (16).

4. With the assistance of the pastor and staff, the director selects members of the catechists of adults team and develops a team vision for the program. The director also begins to train this team in specific adult catechesis skills. The team should include members of the parish staff with a theology and public speaking background (16, 18).

Third Month (September)

1. The director and the two teams begin marketing the adult faith formation vision to the parish (103–111).

2. The adult faith formation team conducts a major needs assessment with the parishioners (104–106).

3. Final decisions based on the major needs assessment produce an overall adult faith formation program for October through the following June (1–2, 25–35, 81–91, 93–101, 113–115). In February and March, the service and community-building components of adult faith formation should receive special planning and marketing attention (93–101).

4. The director and the teams begin marketing the specific program offerings for the mid-October through December semester. Intensive marketing normally precedes each offering by at least one month, with an overall presentation of offerings at the start of each semester or season (for example, fall, winter, spring, summer, including Advent and Lent–Easter special offerings) (103–111).

Fourth Month (October)

1. The fall seminars and other adult faith formation opportunities begin (mid-October through December) (25–35).

2. The director submits to the pastor the first three-month adult faith formation activities report (July–September) (13). The director and the two teams present a Saturday workshop on "Identifying Your Talents for Ministry" to provide new volunteers for both the adult faith formation program and other parish ministries (37–48, 71–80).

3. The director and the two teams begin to assist other parish ministries in developing their adult faith formation skills (13–15, "Applications to Other Parish Ministries" in Chaps. 1–10).

Fifth and Sixth Months (November-December)

1. The director continues to train the two teams in adult catechesis, spirituality, conflict resolution, and other areas of ministry. This includes an evening or day of recollection for both of the teams and the other adult faith formation program volunteers (28–40, 81–91, 59–69).

2. The director and the teams assess the effectiveness of the fall offerings by studying the attendance records and the written evaluations returned by participants (55).

3. The director and the teams plan the winter offerings (January–February, if using a trimester system) or the spring offerings (January–May, if using a semester system) (49–58).

4. Marketing of the winter or spring offerings begins in December. An overall marketing of the entire semester is first provided, and then specific marketing begins one month prior to each individual offering (103–111).

Seventh Month (January)

1. Winter offerings begin (January–February) using the trimester system, or spring offerings begin (January–May) using the semester system (25–35).

2. The director submits the three-month adult faith formation activities report to the pastor (October–December) (13).

3. Director continues to reinforce and empower each team member in his or her unique skills in ministry. This should include individual sessions (37–47).

Eighth Month (February)

1. The director and the two teams market the spring offerings (March–May) if on the trimester system (103–111).

2. With input from the pastor and staff, the director and two teams begin major planning and marketing of the essential all-parishioners service component of the adult catechesis program (7, 93–97).

Ninth Month (March)

1. Spring offerings (March–May) begin if on the trimester system (25–35).

2. The director and two teams, with pastor and staff input, begin major planning and marketing of the essential all-parishioners community-building component of the adult catechesis program (94, 98–99).

Tenth Month (April)

1. The director submits the three-month adult faith formation activities report (January–March) to the pastor (13).

2. The director and two teams provide all possible assistance to the catechumenate and liturgy ministries for a major celebration of the Easter liturgy. The director also provides an evening or day of recollection for both teams and the other adult faith formation program volunteers (113–115, 81–91).

3. Plan summer offerings (for June and July). Leave staggered time off for the director, all team members, and the other volunteers) (49–58).

Eleventh Month (May)

1. Marketing of summer offerings (June–July) begins (103–111).

2. The director and the two teams join with the pastor in the annual adult faith formation program re-visioning weekend retreat to plan for next year (49–58).

3. All team members and other volunteers decide whether to renew or to change their contract of ministry service for the following year. Their decision includes reflection on their skills and the ministry needs (37–47, 71–80).

Twelfth Month (June)

1. Summer offerings (June–July) begin (25–35).

2. At the end of June, the director submits the final three-month adult faith formation activities report (April–June) to the pastor (13).

Bibliography

Ashkar, Dominic F. *Road to Emmaus: A New Model for Catechesis.* San Jose, Calif: Resource Publications, Inc., 1993.

Bacik, James J. *Tensions in the Church: Facing the Challenges, Seizing the Opportunities.* Kansas City, Mo.: Sheed and Ward, 1993.

Baranowski, Arthur R. *Creating Small Church Communities: A Plan for Restructuring the Parish and Renewing Catholic Life.* Cincinnati: St. Anthony Messenger Press, 1993.

Barry, William A., and William J. Connolly. *Finding God in All Things: A Companion to the Spiritual Exercises of St. Ignatius.* Notre Dame, Ind.: Ave Maria Press, 1991.

———. *The Practice of Spiritual Direction.* San Francisco: Harper San Francisco, 1982.

Bausch, William J. *The Total Parish Manual: Everything You Need to Empower Your Faith Community.* Mystic, Conn.: Twenty-third Publications, 1994.

Beckwith, Harry. *The Invisible Touch: The Four Keys to Modern Marketing.* New York: Warner Books, 2000.

Brennan, Patrick J. *Parishes That Excel: Models of Excellence in Education, Ministry and Evangelization.* New York: The Crossroad Publishing Co., 1993.

———. *The Reconciling Parish: A Process for Returning or Alienated Catholics.* Allen, Texas: Thomas More Publishing, 1990.

Brown, Raymond E. *An Introduction to New Testament Christology.* Mahwah, N.J.: Paulist Press, 1994.

Buby, Bertrand. *Mary of Galilee.* Mary in the New Testament series, *vol. 1.* New York: Alba House, 1994.

Burghardt, Walter J. *Preaching: The Art and the Craft.* Mahwah, N.J.: Paulist Press, 1987.

Congregation for the Clergy. *General Directory for Catechesis.* Washington, D.C.: United States Catholic Conference, 1997.

Congregation for the Evangelization of Peoples. *Guide for Catechists.* Washington, D.C.: United States Catholic Conference, 1994.

Connell, Martin, ed. *The Catechetical Documents: A Parish Resource.* Chicago: Liturgy Training Publications, 1996.

Crosby, Michael H. *The Dysfunctional Church: Addiction and Codependency in the Family of Catholicism.* Notre Dame, Ind.: Ave Maria Press, 1991.

Department of Education, United States Catholic Conference. *Groundwork: Cultivating Adult Religious Education in the Parish, A Workshop Design*. Washington, D.C.: United States Catholic Conference, 1990.

———. *Leader's Guide to* Our Hearts Were Burning Within Us. Washington, D.C.: United States Catholic Conference, 2000.

———. *Serving Life and Faith: Adult Religious Education and the American Catholic Community*. Washington, D.C.: United States Catholic Conference, 1986.

Dolan, Jay P., and Allan Figueroa Deck, eds. *Hispanic Catholic Culture in the U.S.: Issues and Concerns*. vol 3. Notre Dame, Ind.: University of Notre Dame Press, 1994.

Dougherty, Rose Mary. *Group Spiritual Direction: Community for Discernment*. Mahwah, N.J.: Paulist Press, 1995.

Gallagher, Maureen. *The Art of Catechesis: What You Need to Be, Know and Do*. Mahwah, N.J.: Paulist Press, 1998.

Gelpi, Donald L. *The Conversion Experience: A Reflective Process for RCIA Participants*. Mahwah, N.J.: Paulist Press, 1998.

Gillen, Marie A., and Maurice C. Taylor, eds. *Adult Religious Education: A Journey of Faith Development*. Mahwah, N.J.: Paulist Press, 1995.

Green, Thomas H. *Come Down Zacchaeus: Spirituality and the Laity*. Notre Dame, Ind.: Ave Maria Press, 1988.

Groome, Thomas H. *Educating for Life: A Spiritual Vision for Every Teacher and Parent*. Allen, Texas: Thomas More Publishing, 1998.

Haring, Bernard. *My Hope for the Church: Critical Encouragement for the Twenty-First Century*. Ligouri, Mo.: Ligouri Publications, 1999.

Hater, Robert J. *Parish Catechetical Ministry*. Mission Hills, Calif.: Benziger, 1986.

Heney, David. *Motivating Your Parish to Change: Concrete Leadership Strategies for Pastors, Administrators, and Lay Leaders*. San Jose, Calif.: Resource Publications, Inc., 1998.

Hopkins, Tom. *How to Master the Art of Selling*. New York: Warner Books, 1982.

International Council for Catechesis. *Adult Catechesis in the Christian Community: Some Principles and Guidelines*. Washington, D.C.: United States Catholic Conference, 1992.

John Paul II. *The Lay Members of Christ's Faithful People*. Boston: Pauline Books and Media, 1988.

Jorgensen, Susan S. *Eucharist! An Eight-Session Ritual-Catechesis Experience for Adults*. San Jose, Calif.: Resource Publications, Inc., 1994.

Karasik, Paul. *How to Make It Big in the Seminar Business*. New York: McGraw-Hill, 1992.

Kavanaugh, Kieran, and Otilio Rodriguez, trans. *The Collected Works of St. John of the Cross*. Washington, D.C.: ICS Publications, 1991.

———. *The Collected Works of St. Teresa of Avila.* Vol. 1. 2nd ed. Washington, D.C.: ICS Publications, Institute of Carmelite Studies, 1987.

———. *The Collected Works of St. Teresa of Avila.* Vol. 2. Washington, D.C.: ICS Publications, Institute of Carmelite Studies, 1980.

Keating, Thomas. *Open Mind, Open Heart: The Contemplative Dimension of the Gospel.* New York: The Continuum International Publishing Group, 1995.

Kleissler, Thomas A., Margo A. LeBert, and Mary C. McGuinness. *Small Christian Communities: A Vision of Hope for the 21st Century.* Mahwah, N.J.: Paulist Press, 1991.

Knaus, William J. *Do It Now: How to Stop Procrastinating.* Englewood Cliffs, N.J.: Prentice-Hall Inc., 1979.

Kramer, Marilynn. *The Marilynn Kramer Story: Joy Comes in the Morning.* Ann Arbor Mich.: Servant Publications, 1990.

Levinson, Jay Conrad. *Guerilla Marketing: Secrets for Making Big Profits from Your Small Business.* Boston: Houghton Mifflin Co., 1984.

Lyons, Enda. *Jesus: Self-Portrait by God.* Mahwah, N.J.: Paulist Press, 1994.

McBrien, Richard P. *Catholicism.* San Francisco: Harper San Francisco, 1981.

———. *Ministry: A Theological, Pastoral Handbook.* San Francisco: Harper San Francisco, 1987.

McKinney, Mary Benet. *Sharing Wisdom: A Process for Group Decision Making.* Allen, Texas: Thomas More Publishing, 1987.

Megargee, Edwin Inglee. *The California Psychological Inventory Handbook.* San Francisco: Jossey-Bass, Inc., 1977.

Miller, Lew. *Your Divine Connection: Prayer Through Mental Imagery.* Millbrae, Calif.: Celestial Arts, 1977.

Mongoven, Ann Marie. *The Prophetic Spirit of Catechesis: How We Share the Fire in Our Hearts.* Mahwah, N.J.: Paulist Press, 2000.

Morris, Thomas H. *The RCIA: Transforming the Church, A Resource for Pastoral Implementation.* New York.: Paulist Press, 1989.

National Conference of Catholic Bishops. *Hispanic Ministry: Three Major Documents.* Washington, D.C.: United States Catholic Conference, 1995.

Peck, M. Scott. *People of the Lie: The Hope for Healing Human Evil.* New York: Simon & Schuster, Inc., 1983.

Pinsoneault, Donna. *Attracting and Managing Volunteers: A Parish Handbook.* Liguori, Mo.: Liguori Publications, 2001.

Rahner, Karl, and Bruce W. Gilette, trans. *The Need and the Blessing of Prayer: A New Translation of Father Rahner's Book on Prayer.* Collegeville, Minn.: The Liturgical Press, 1997.

Ratcliff, Donald, and Blake J. Neff. *The Complete Guide to Religious Education Volunteers.* Birmingham, Ala.: Religious Education Press, 1993.

Robbins, Anthony. *Awaken the Giant Within: How to Take Immediate Control of Your Mental, Emotional, Physical and Financial Destiny.* New York: Fireside, 1992.

Rucker, Kathy D. *Adult Education in the Parish: A Practical Handbook.* Cincinnati: St. Anthony Messenger Press, 1990.

Shawchuck, Norman, et al. *Marketing for Congregations: Choosing to Serve People More Effectively.* Nashville: Abingdon Press, 1992.

Tighe, Jeanne, and Karen Szentkeresti. *Rethinking Adult Religious Education: A Practical Parish Guide.* Mahwah, N.J.: Paulist Press, 1986.

Whitehead, James D., and Evelyn Eaton Whitehead. *Method in Ministry: Theological Reflection and Christian Ministry.* San Francisco: Harper Collins Publishers, 1980.

Wilkes, Paul. *Excellent Catholic Parishes: The Guide to Best Places and Practices.* Mahwah, N.J.: Paulist Press, 2001.

Wilson, Marlene. *How to Mobilize Church Volunteers.* Minneapolis: Augsburg Books, 1983.

Zimmerman, Joyce Ann, et al. *Living Liturgy: Spirituality, Celebration, Catechesis, Sundays and Solemnities. Year C—2001.* Collegeville, Minn.: The Liturgical Press, 2000.

Resources for Faith Formation

CELEBRATING THE LECTIONARY
Adult packet
Edited by Cathy Qualls
Looseleaf, 3-hole punched, 500 pages, 8½" x 11"
Materials for September through August

With *Celebrating the Lectionary's* Adult packet, participants or volunteer leaders can organize a weekly one-hour session for adults based on the Sunday lectionary. This catechetical resource has everything you need: seasonal and Sunday backgrounds, session plans, photocopiable handouts, color posters and more. Use these materials for catechumenate sessions, lector preparation or parent sessions conducted in concert with a children's program. Also contains catechumenate dismissal questions and Cycle A Scrutiny Sunday sessions.

INTRODUCING LITURGICAL CATECHESIS
Formation Sessions for the Parish
Nick Wagner
80 pages, 8½" x 11", ISBN 0-89390-566-6

With *Introducing Liturgical Catechesis,* you can immerse your pastoral team in both the concepts and the methods of liturgical catechesis. These photocopiable training sessions will make liturgical catechesis a reality in your parish. Contains reflection questions and a bibliography.

Order these books from your local bookseller
or call 1-888-273-7782 (toll-free) or 1-408-286-8505
or visit the Resource Publications, Inc., website at www.rpinet.com.

More Resources for Faith Formation

BULLETIN INSERTS FOR LITURGICAL CATECHESIS
Marion Eagen
Illustrated by Mike Sagara
CD-ROM; Text, tiff and pdf files; UPC 784967-003723/ISBN 0-89390-568-2

Looking for an easy way to support your catechetical efforts? Use your bulletin! With *Bulletin Inserts for Liturgical Catechesis*, you can choose from more than 130 short articles explaining the liturgical year, special feasts and solemnities, the liturgical books and important symbols and concepts. You have the option of selecting the item as a text file, so that you can manipulate it in your word processor program, or as a fully formatted insert. Includes graphics for each item.

ML BULLETIN INSERTS VOLUMES 1 AND 2
Paul Turner
Illustrations by George F. Collopy
CD-ROM, Text, tiff and pdf files, ISBN 0-89390-590-9

This resource contains 160 inserts in two volumes or e-books — one with 80 inserts from the first volume of *ML Bulletin Inserts* and another adding 80 more inserts. These short, informative comments on liturgical topics will help answer questions that your assembly has about the liturgy. Each of the inserts includes accompanying clip art. The electronic format gives you different options for importing the inserts into your bulletin. A comprehensive index and full permission to reprint is included.

Order these books from your local bookseller
or call 1-888-273-7782 (toll-free) or 1-408-286-8505
or visit the Resource Publications, Inc., website at www.rpinet.com.

"What Every Catholic Needs to Know..."

WHAT EVERY CATHOLIC NEEDS TO KNOW
ABOUT LENT, TRIDUUM, AND EASTER
A Parish Guide to the Paschal Season
Kevin McGloin
48 pages, 5½" x 8½", ISBN 0-89390-540-2

What Every Catholic Needs to Know about Lent, Triduum, and Easter walks the average Catholic through the history of the season, its liturgy, and prayers and activities they can do in their own homes. Great for liturgy committees, catechumenate groups, adult study groups and the entire parish. Bulk discounts available.

WHAT EVERY CATHOLIC NEEDS TO KNOW
ABOUT THE MASS
A Parish Guide to Liturgy
Kevin McGloin
80 pages, 5½" x 8½", ISBN 0-89390-536-4

What Every Catholic Needs to Know about the Mass walks the average Catholic through the history of liturgy, their role in the Mass, the importance of art and environment, the place of music and a vision of what liturgy would be like if the whole assembly took their roles seriously. Great for liturgy committees, catechumenate groups, adult study groups and the entire parish. Bulk discounts available.

WHAT EVERY CATHOLIC NEEDS TO KNOW
ABOUT ADVENT AND CHRISTMAS
A Parish Guide to the Incarnation Season
Kevin McGloin
48 pages, 5½" x 8½", ISBN 0-89390-549-6

How can you make Christmas more than a commercial holiday punctuated by a bit of church time? *What Every Catholic Needs to Know about Advent and Christmas* will help. This little book walks the average Catholic through the history of the season, its liturgy, and prayers and activities they can do in their own homes. Great for liturgy committees, catechumenate groups, adult study groups and the entire parish. Bulk discounts available.

Order these books from your local bookseller
or call 1-888-273-7782 (toll-free) or 1-408-286-8505
or visit the Resource Publications, Inc., website at www.rpinet.com.

Try this popular series for your ministry.

MODERN LITURGY ANSWERS THE 101 MOST-ASKED QUESTIONS ABOUT LITURGY
Nick Wagner
144 pages, 5½" x 8½", ISBN 0-89390-369-8

Everyone has a question about liturgy. Get answers from this authoritative work. You'll learn the historical and theological background of current liturgical practices and you'll get practical solutions to vexing pastoral problems. Use this important reference book for your planning or to provide quick authoritative answers.

THE CATHOLIC WEDDING ANSWER BOOK
ML Answers the 101 Most-Asked Questions series
Paul Turner
160 pages, 5½" x 8½", ISBN 0-89390-517-8

This book will help you catechize engaged couples, find solutions to pastoral dilemmas and set sensitive wedding guidelines that are grounded firmly in Catholic liturgical tradition. Because this book covers 101 frequently asked questions, you may want to get every engaged couple in your parish a copy of this book before they start planning their wedding.

THE LITURGICAL MUSIC ANSWER BOOK
ML Answers the 101 Most-Asked Questions series
Peggy Lovrien
160 pages, 5½" x 8½", ISBN 0-89390-454-6

Here is a virtual training manual for music directors, song leaders and choir members. The *Liturgical Music Answer Book* helps parish liturgical music committees study the liturgical music documents of the church, discover the appropriate ways to choose music for the liturgy and operate with confidence in their ministry as liturgical musicians.

THE CATECHUMENATE ANSWER BOOK
ML Answers the 101 Most-Asked Questions series
Paul Turner
160 pages, 5½" x 8½", ISBN 0-89390-501-1

This book answers 101 questions that range from the basic to the historical and from the practical to the catechetical. Use this authoritative work to answer questions from catechumens, find solutions to pastoral dilemmas, generate ideas for the celebration of the rites and ensure your catechumenal process is going in the right direction.

Order these books from your local bookseller
or call 1-888-273-7782 (toll-free) or 1-408-286-8505
or visit the Resource Publications, Inc., website at www.rpinet.com.